The Gingerbread Book

The
Gingerbread Book

STEVEN STELLINGWERF

RIZZOLI
NEW YORK

To Deb and Jenna

First published in the United States of America in 1991 by
RIZZOLI INTERNATIONAL PUBLICATIONS, INC
300 Park Avenue South, New York, NY 10010

First published in the United Kingdom in 1991 by
Charles Letts & Co Ltd
Diary House, Borough Road
London SE1 1DW
England

Library of Congress Cataloging-in-Publication Data
Stellingwerf. Steven.
    The gingerbread book/Steven Stellingwerf.
      p. cm.
    ISBN 0–8478–1414–9
     1. Gingerbread. 2. Gingerbread houses. I. Title.
    TX771.S746 1991   91–52793
    641.8′653–dc20   CIP

"Letts" is a registered trademark of
Charles Letts (Scotland) Ltd

Editorial Director: Joanna Lorenz
Art Director: Peter Bridgewater
Text Editor: Lewis Esson
Designers: Mike Snell, Ron Bryant-Funnell
Photographer: Alan Newnham

Printed and bound in Hong Kong

Contents

Introduction

As a child growing up in a predominantly Dutch community in America, I recall visiting the local bakery with my sister on Saturday mornings. We couldn't wait to see the variety of tempting pastries and cookies that lined the bakery cases. One treat we often purchased was a gingerbread cookie, shaped as a windmill and decorated with almonds. We both enjoyed the distinctively spicy yet mild flavour. One Saturday, shortly before Christmas, we returned to the bakery to find that our favourite cookies were now in a different shape. They were no longer windmills, but had become men with raisin eyes and buttons. We tried them eagerly, and to our surprise only the shape had changed, not the taste.

Upon leaving the bakery with our sack of gingerbread men, I caught sight of an enchanting village in the front window of the bakery, composed of several brightly decorated gingerbread houses. I was captivated by the houses with their multitude of brilliantly coloured Christmas candies, cookies and icing. Each house had a chocolate pathway leading to the front door, with a gingerbread man standing to one side ready to greet visitors. The whole village was covered with a light dusting of sugar to represent snow. I stood there mesmerized, wondering how someone could have created all this.

This was my first exposure to the art of gingerbread-making. Little did I realize that, years later, I would be writing a book on this centuries-old art form.

It is surprisingly simple to build a magical centrepiece from gingerbread. In this book, I aim to provide beginners with the basic knowledge and skills needed to create a gingerbread project and give new inspiration to those with more experience.

The book contains information on all the equipment you will need, most of which is probably already in your kitchen. There are detailed instructions on basic techniques, from rolling out the gingerbread dough to simple piping ideas which can be used to decorate your project. The five main chapters each consist of several projects, ranging from simple cut-outs to more elaborate centrepieces for special-occasion parties. The projects towards the end of the book need a little more understanding of the skills involved, but not much. I also include, of course, my favourite recipes for the gingerbread dough and icings needed to construct the projects.

Throughout my involvement with gingerbread, I have realized that most people think that it is something which is only suitable for the Christmas season. I make gingerbread all the year round and the book contains ideas for Easter, Hallowe'en, St. Valentine's Day, birthdays as well as Christmas. You will find that just by altering the colour and decorations of a specific project you can change it from an item suitable for one occasion to another.

I hope this book provides you with many hours of fun and enjoyment and will inspire you to create gingerbread all year round.

STEVEN STELLINGWERF

The History of Gingerbread

Crisp flat cookies cut into the shape of men and women, animals or hearts, diamonds and stars, which are sometimes iced or stamped in moulds and may be built into heavily decorated festive houses; dry, delicately spiced loaves or small cakes; thick cookies, semi-soft or crisp, also iced by some bakers; deliciously sticky, moist squares of cake, sometimes eaten with soured cream, apple-sauce or cheese: all these are rightly called 'gingerbread'.

The term may be imprecise because, in Medieval England, gingerbread meant simply 'preserved ginger' and was a corruption of the Old French *gingebras* derived from the Latin name for the spice, *Zingebar*. It was only in the fifteenth century that the term came to be applied to a kind of cake made with treacle and flavoured with ginger. Before long the original use of the term gave way to the new one, but 'gingerbread' is still used to refer to sweet cakes differing widely in substance but almost all made with some variation on the combination of ginger with treacle, molasses or honey.

Ginger

The generic name for ginger comes from the Sanskrit – *sringavera*, meaning 'root shaped like a horn' (strictly it is a rhizome) because of its passing resemblance to an animal horn. The origins of the spice lie in Asia, though now it is mostly grown in Jamaica. The ancient Chinese used it as a medical treatment and it was mentioned by Confucius (*c*.551–479 BC) in his *Analects*. The Romans used it extensively and taxed it heavily – it almost certainly came overland from India. With the fall of the Roman Empire the supply to Europe almost dried up and the spice only became freely available again after the Venetian explorer Marco Polo brought it back from the Far East at the end of the thirteenth century. The widespread passion for spices in Medieval Europe (partly to cover up the taste of meats preserved through the winter without the benefits of refrigeration) included ginger, and the spice merchants took advantage by charging high prices. Ginger was the second most highly traded spice after pepper.

Ginger was also discovered to have a preservative effect when added to breads and pastries, and this probably led to the development of recipes for ginger cakes and breads.

Ginger also became valued in Europe for its medicinal benefits. Henry VIII sent the Lord Mayor of London a ginger-based recipe to help build the body's resistance to the plague which was then endemic in Europe. Its present-day use in remedies for travel sickness was anticipated by John Baret in his *Alvearie or triple dictionarie* of 1573–80: 'A Kinde of cake or paste made to comfort the stomacke: ginger bread, *mustaceum*.'

Gingerbread

The manufacture of gingerbread appears to have spread throughout western Europe at the end of the eleventh century, possibly introduced by crusaders returning from wars in the Eastern Mediterranean. From its very beginnings gingerbread has been a fairground delicacy. Hard biscuits cut into pretty shapes of kings and queens, animals or letters of the alphabet – often gilded – were as much a feature of Medieval fairs in France, Germany, Holland and England as jousting tournaments, fluttering flags and performing bears. Many fairs became known as 'gingerbread fairs' and ginger-bread items took on the alternative name in England of 'fairings' – which had the generic meaning of a gift given at, or brought from, a fair. Certain shapes were associated with different seasons: buttons and flowers were found at Easter fairs and animals and birds were a feature in autumn. The gingerbread was often decorated to resemble the armour of the day – studded with gilded cloves to look like golden nails and small box leaves arranged in the pattern of a fleur-de-lis.

In Paris a gingerbread fair was held from the eleventh century until the nineteenth at an Abbey on the site of the present St. Antoine Hospital, where the monks sold ginger-bread cut into the shape of pigs. In England, among the many

'When they went close up to the cottage, they saw that it was made of gingerbread and cake, and that the windows were made of clear sugar. Hansel reached up and broke a piece of the roof, to see how it tasted.' From Grimm's Fairy Tales, *illustrated by Anne Anderson in 1928.*

fairs known as 'gingerbread fairs', were two held from the thirteenth century until the twentieth in Birmingham, one at Whitsun and the other at Michaelmas.

Gingerbread became synonymous in England with something pretty and showy. In 1708, William King wrote of 'the enticing gold of gingerbread' (*The Art of Cookery, in imitation of Horace's Art of Poetry*) and the expression 'to take the gilt off the gingerbread' is still common today, even if gilded gingerbread is now rarely seen. Sailors would describe the carved and gilded decoration of their ships as 'gingerbread work'. From this usage the term even came to be applied to the style of architectural detail so common on houses in colonial seaports, featuring extensive carved and fretted wooden ornamentation.

The tradition of cutting gingerbread into human shapes still survives in the form of gingerbread men with eyes and buttons made from currants or raisins. Queen Elizabeth I is supposed to have commanded gingerbread cut into caricatures of her courtiers, but there is more than one village tradition in England requiring the unmarried women to eat gingerbread 'husbands' at the fair if they are to stand a good chance of meeting a real husband. In Belgium, gingerbread *spéculos* are cut into folk characters such as Harlequin, Columbine and St. Nicholas. In eighteenth-century England, gingerbread alphabet letters were as familiar as gingerbread men. In *The Expedition of Humphry Clinker*, Tobias Smollett has the entry '3 June, She don't yet know her letters . . . but I will bring her the ABC in gingerbread.' Moulds were also used to shape gingerbread into windmills or castles, kings, queens and animals.

The European Tradition

The French version of gingerbread is *pain d'épice*, or spice bread, made with honey and spices. The Guild of *Pain d'épiciers*, founded in Reims, received official recognition from Henry IV in 1596, but for all its later royal approval it does not appear in *Le Viandier* – the first French cookbook written by Taillevant, the fourteenth-century cook to Charles VI – it was a peasant delicacy far beneath his notice.

There are two types of gingerbread commonly made in France: the gingerbread of Dijon in Burgundy – no man was famous until he had been portrayed in Dijon gingerbread – which was made with wheat flour and egg yolks; and *couque* made with rye flour. According to Larousse, the traditional method was to mix the spices and sweeteners together and leave them to mature in a cool dry place for several months before the remaining ingredients were added and the gingerbread was shaped and baked. Today *pain d'épice* is usually sold as a dryish loaf or small cakes.

The cookery writer Waverley Root argues that the English retained a passion for ginger long after the rest of Medieval Europe had tired of it, and certainly there are many English variations on the gingerbread theme that are still popular. 'Cornish Fairings', a relic of the many fairings baked for fairs all over England, are cookie-like, sweetened with honey and decorated with almonds, marzipan, icing and gold leaf. They are particularly linked to a fair held at the market town of Launceston just after Christmas, but there are also records of gingerbreads being sold at fairs in Widdecombe, Norwich and Cambridge.

The king of the sticky, cake-like gingerbreads made in England is Yorkshire Parkin, eaten traditionally on Guy Fawkes Day (November 5th). Fawkes, whose failure to blow up the King as he opened Parliament in 1605 is celebrated with fireworks and bonfires, was born in York in 1570 and this may explain the connection. Yorkshire Parkin is made with treacle (cheaper than sugar and consumed in larger quantities in the less prosperous north of England than in the south) and oatmeal. Before ovens became widespread, parkin was cooked on the hearthstone and was sometimes known as 'tharve cake' from 'the hearth cake'. Both parkin and gingerbread were kept in specially made wooden boxes. 'Mulatto's

Gingerbread was a traditional part of the cook's repertoire in Germany in the 18th century, and there were special 'gingerbread-bakers' in every town.

stomach' is an especially rich variant on the parkin theme, made with molasses and sour milk.

Grasmere gingerbread is another festive gingerbread, made in the Lake District home of poet William Wordsworth. Like a cross between a cookie and a sponge cake, it is traditionally shaped into a likeness of St. Oswald for the rush-bearing ceremony held at the beginning of August on the Saturday nearest to St. Oswald's Day. Rushes are strewn on the floor of the church and the children taking part in the festivities are presented with pieces of gingerbread.

Of all the countries in Europe, Germany is the one with the longest and strongest tradition of flat shaped gingerbreads. At every autumn fair in Germany, and in the lands around where the Germanic influence is strong, there are rows of stalls filled with hundreds of gingerbread hearts decorated with white and coloured icing and tied with ribbons.

In Nürnberg in northern Bavaria, *lebkuchen* flavoured with ginger have been made for more than 600 years. This was a natural result of the combined presence in the region of abundant honey and a prosperous spice trade carried on by *Pfeffersäcke* – 'peppersacks' – the spice merchants. Nürnberg gingerbread was not baked in the home, but was the preserve of an exclusive Guild of master bakers, the *Lebkuchler*.

Lebkuchen (not always flavoured with ginger, but invariably spiced) are made throughout Germany and large pieces of lebkuchen are used to build *Hexenhäusle* – witches' houses (from the fairy tale *Hansel and Gretel*), also called *Lebkuchenhäusle* and *Knusperhäuschen* ('houses for nibbling at'). There are also traditions of making gingerbread men in Germany. According to one story, the landlord of the eighteenth-century poet Gotthold Ephraim Lessing, who was then living in Breslau, made a gingerbread caricature of his dissolute young lodger in an attempt to shame him into mending his rowdy ways. In the Medieval Prussian university town of Torun, now part of Poland, iced flat oblong pieces of gingerbread with rounded ends, called 'Little Kates', are still made.

Throughout Scandinavia, spiced honey cakes similar to *lebkuchen* are made into festive houses at Christmas time.

Gingerbread in the New World

Gingerbread making in North America has its origins in the traditions of the many settlers from all parts of northern Europe who brought with them family recipes and customs.

Ginger was first introduced by the English colonists and the spice speedily became popular. Waverley Root reports that 'ginger cookies were among the goodies passed out to the incorruptible voters of Virginia to induce them to choose the correct candidate for the House of Burgesses.' Molasses, an almost invariable ingredient of American gingerbreads both soft and hard, was described by John Adams as an 'essential ingredient to American independence' (referring to the contentious 1733 Molasses Act which imposed high duties on molasses imported from other than English islands). There are recipes for gingerbread made with maple syrup, but these are much less common.

Gingerbread's earliest home in North America was New England. The first genuinely American cookbook – *American Cookery* by Amelia Simmons published in Hartford, Connecticut in 1796 – contains a recipe for a cake-like molasses gingerbread. Bill Neal in *Biscuits, Spoonbread and Sweet Potato Pie* (1990), gives a Virginian recipe for 'Racy Gingerbread' – a cake-like gingerbread, requiring six races (roots) of ginger, which is cut into squares and iced with whipped cream. He suggests this may be traced back to a traditional Scotch cake of oatmeal, treacle and green ginger, something very like parkin.

The Pennsylvania Dutch were German-speaking immigrants (Dutch is a corruption of 'deutsch', meaning folk in German) from the valley of the Rhine who migrated to the south-eastern part of the new colony of Pennsylvania in the eighteenth century to escape lands devastated by war. They brought with them recipes for German *lebkuchen* and these now exist in many forms, some of them containing no ginger. They may be either soft cakes cut into squares, or dough which is chilled overnight and then rolled out and cut into hearts or diamonds and baked until crisp and then iced.

The unmistakable portent of autumn smoke and falling leaves carried by gingerbread is recalled by Helen Walker Linsenmayer in her record of cooking in Southern Illinois *Cooking Plain* (1976). 'Gingerbread and fresh cider heralded the coming of autumn in my childhood, and we continued to request this spicy dessert through the winter. It was a welcome addition to our school lunch boxes. Bites were taken alternately with crisp apple chunks.' Her hardy ancestors were of both German and British stock.

A gingerbread stamp from New England, America, with the distinctive design of an Indian chief (c.1820, now in the Old Sturbridge Village collection).

Mrs Washington's Gingerbread

½ cup/4oz/115g butter
½ cup/4oz/115g dark brown moist sugar
½ cup/6oz/170g treacle or molasses
½ cup/6oz/170g golden syrup
½ cup/4fl oz/100 ml warm milk
2 tbsp ground ginger
1½ tsp ground cinnamon
1½ tsp ground mace
1½ tsp grated nutmeg
3 tbsp cooking sherry
1 tsp cream of tartar
3 cups/12oz/350g plain flour
3 eggs, well beaten
juice and grated zest of 1 large orange
1 tsp bicarbonate of soda, dissolved in 2 tbsp of warm water
1 cup sultanas or raisins

Different writers have varying opinions about what is the more 'American' style of gingerbread, soft or hard. William Woys Weaver in *American Eats* (1989) says that 'Because of our climate, we tend to make our gingerbreads much harder than the English or Continental Europeans.' Susan Purdy in *A Piece of Cake* (1989), on the other hand, describes Amelia Simmons' recipe as 'the first published recipe for American soft-style gingerbread, which departed from the more traditional crisp, cookie-like European gingerbread.' The truth is that there are as many different recipes for gingerbread – snaps, cookies, cakes and sweet breads – as there are cooks.

The recipes used in this book are for the 'hard' gingerbreads used to make houses, but one of the best recipes for 'soft' gingerbread on either side of the Atlantic is attributed to President George Washington's mother, Mary Ball Washington. According to the curators of the American Museum at Bath in England, 'This recipe was found in an old worn cookery book. Many of Mary Washington's descendants have this same recipe. When the Marquis de Lafayette visited his beloved friend, George Washington, he went to call on Washington's mother. Although she was raking leaves in the garden, she greeted them unaffectedly and went into the house to make a mint julep with which she served a well-spiced gingerbread. Listening with pleased attention to the Frenchman's praises of her son, her only reply was "George was always a good boy"!'

● Cream the butter with the sugar and beat well. Add the syrups, milk, spices and sherry and mix very well. Sift the cream of tartar with the flour and add this mixture alternately with the beaten egg to the butter mixture, mixing in each addition well. Add orange juice and grated zest and dissolved soda and raisins.

● Pour into a well-greased baking pan, about 12 × 9 × 3 in/30 × 23 × 7.5 cm, and bake in a moderate oven (350°F/180°C/gas 4) for 45–50 minutes.

In America, as in Europe, gingerbread is associated with festivals and fairs. One New England recipe is known variously as 'Muster Day', 'Training Day' or 'Election Day' gingerbread, or 'Training Cakes'. These were flat cookies cut with biscuit cutters or stamped with carved wooden moulds or 'prints'. The moulds usually depicted patriotic themes: before the Revolution these were generally the King or Governor; after Independence, the American Eagle. The cookies were handed out on the days when the county militias gathered for the election of officers or for the military training of all men aged between eighteen and forty-five. The militia men were accompanied on such occasions by their wives, children and other relatives who turned the day into a family celebration.

The harder gingerbreads also featured at more sombre occasions in the form of moulded biscuits served after funerals. Caraway or tansy seeds were usually added.

At Christmas, gingerbread makes its most impressive appearance. The German practice of making *lebkuchen* houses never caught on in Britain in the same way as it did in North America, and it is here still that the most extraordinary creations are found. Elaborate Victorian houses, heavy with candies and sugar icicles, vie in competition with Hansel and Gretel houses, more richly decorated and ornamented than most children could imagine in their wildest dreams.

Ingredients and Recipes

There are a few things to remember when selecting the ingredients for your gingerbread recipe:

Ginger is only one of the many spices and ingredients which go into gingerbread dough. There are many hundreds of recipes for gingerbread and in parts of Europe and America the recipes will vary from city to city and family to family. Some recipes are handed down from generation to generation and guarded fiercely. The gingerbread recipes I am sharing with you are my two favourites: they are easy to work, taste delicious, and the baked pieces keep their shape and have a good natural gloss to them. All the ingredients can be found in any grocery store, supermarket or health-food shop and you will probably have the basics like flour, sugar, and eggs in the kitchen already. Remember that it is important to use the freshest available.

You will notice when comparing most gingerbread recipes that they all call for similar ingredients, but the quantities of these ingredients will vary from recipe to recipe. Different amounts of each ingredient will change the gingerbread dough slightly. For example, the recipe on page 15 calls for a smaller quantity of baking soda than most, but I find that gingerbread pieces baked with this recipe tend to hold their shape much better than others. I therefore use this recipe for the more detailed projects, such as **Jack-in-the-Box** (page 76).

Eggs

Most recipes call for large to extra-large eggs and they should be the freshest available. The eggs should be well beaten before being added to the mixture, to ensure that they are evenly mixed in.

Spices

You will notice that in some gingerbread recipes the only spice used is ginger, whereas others may include as many as five different spices. Ginger is a very light-coloured, relatively mild-flavoured spice. If ginger alone is used in a recipe, the finished product will stay a light colour with just a hint of the spice flavour to it. Recipes with more spices added to them have a darker colour and a much more pungent flavour.

Sugar

Ordinary white sugar works best in most recipes. If a recipe calls for brown sugar there is usually a choice between light and dark. The light will obviously result in a paler gingerbread, whereas the dark will deepen the colour.

Molasses

Molasses can be purchased at most grocery stores, supermarkets or health-food shops (it is regarded as a natural sweetener). As with brown sugar, there are light and dark varieties, but the difference in colour is more noticeable. The light molasses gives a pale golden-brown dough with a dull finish when baked. Dark molasses gives the dough a rich dark colour and a glossy finish when baked.

Flour

The flour used in the recipes may be either white or wholewheat, whichever you prefer. The use of either will slightly affect the flavour of the gingerbread but not its workability.

If you choose self-raising flour (which contains baking powder) your pieces will rise a little while baking, but they will return to their original thickness when removed from the oven. You will also find that they will spread out slightly and will need to be trimmed as soon as they come out of the oven, before they cool and set.

Basic Gingerbread

RECIPE 1

1½ cups/3½oz/100g flour
1 tbsp ground ginger
4 tbsp light molasses
3 tbsp light brown sugar
¼ cup/2oz/50g butter
½ tsp baking soda
1 egg, beaten

● Preheat the oven to 350°F/180°C/gas 4.
● In a large mixing bowl, sift the flour and ginger together. In a saucepan, combine molasses, brown sugar and butter. Heat slowly, stirring occasionally, until thoroughly melted. Stir the baking soda into the melted mixture and then add this to the flour mixture along with the beaten egg and mix to a dough.
● Knead the dough on a floured surface until it is smooth and free from cracks. Roll and cut or mould into shape and bake for 10–20 minutes, until a light golden brown.

Old-Fashioned Gingerbread

RECIPE 2

5 cups/12oz/350g flour
1 tsp baking soda
1 tsp salt
1 tsp each cloves and nutmeg
2 tsp each cinnamon and ginger
1 cup/8oz/225g vegetable shortening
1 cup/8oz/225g sugar
1¼ cups/6oz/170g molasses
2 eggs, beaten

● Preheat the oven to 350°F/180°C/gas 4.
● In a large bowl, blend together the flour, baking soda, salt and spices. In a saucepan, melt the shortening over a gentle heat. Cool slightly until lukewarm, then pour into the bowl of a food processor and add the sugar, molasses and eggs. Blend on medium speed until mixed well, scraping the sides of the bowl occasionally. Mix in the dry ingredients thoroughly.
● Roll and cut or mould into shape and bake for 15–20 minutes, until the edges are slightly brown.

Royal Icing

Makes 3 cups/1¼lb/550g
3 cups/1lb/450g icing/confectioners' sugar, sifted
2 tbsp meringue powder (albumen powder)
6–7 tbsp warm water

● In a spotlessly clean and grease-free mixing bowl, combine the sugar and the meringue powder. Add the water and beat until the icing forms peaks (about 8–10 minutes with a heavy-duty mixer, 10–12 minutes with a hand-held mixer).
● Keep the icing covered with a damp cloth while it is being used and store it in an airtight container (there is no need to refrigerate it). Rebeat at low speed before using again.
● NOTE: For successful icing, keep all utensils *completely* grease-free.
● When colouring icing, always add a little pigment at a time as it is easy to add more colour and very difficult to remove it.
● When making up batches of coloured icing, always make a generous amount as it can be very difficult to duplicate a matching shade of colour exactly if you run out in the middle of the decoration.

Fresh Egg-White Royal Icing

Makes 2½ cups/1lb/450g
white of 1 large egg, at room temperature
2½ cups/10oz/285g icing/confectioners' sugar, sifted
pinch of cream of tartar (tartaric acid)

● Place the egg white in a large bowl. Gradually stir in half the sugar with the cream of tartar until the mixture is the consistency of unwhipped cream. Add the remaining sugar, a spoonful at a time, stirring thoroughly after each addition.
● Stir, but do not beat, until the icing stands in firm peaks when the spoon is lifted out.

Decorations

The most important aspect of your gingerbread construction! It is the decorative piping and embellishment with sweets and candies that make a gingerbread house so irresistible.

When selecting sweets and candies, a subtle choice of complementary colourways is to my mind much more effective than a complete riot of colour – unless, of course, this is the theme of the creation! A classic Hansel and Gretel gingerbread cottage is traditionally encrusted with colourful sweets, and this is part of its appeal. But by just choosing to decorate a gingerbread building with, for example, dark and white chocolate truffles, and keeping the piping to white and red, a completely different, very sophisticated effect is achieved. Every sweet and candy store presents countless possibilities and inspirations.

Candies and sweets vary from country to country, but in my travels I have always found that if the exact sweet you are looking for is not available, there is always a similar one suitable for substitution. And you are not restricted to sweets, either – nuts, raisins, biscuits, and even sugar and cereal squares have all been used in this book to represent parts of the construction.

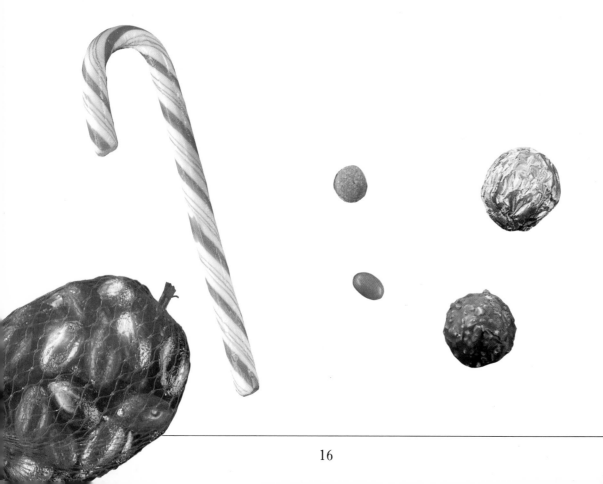

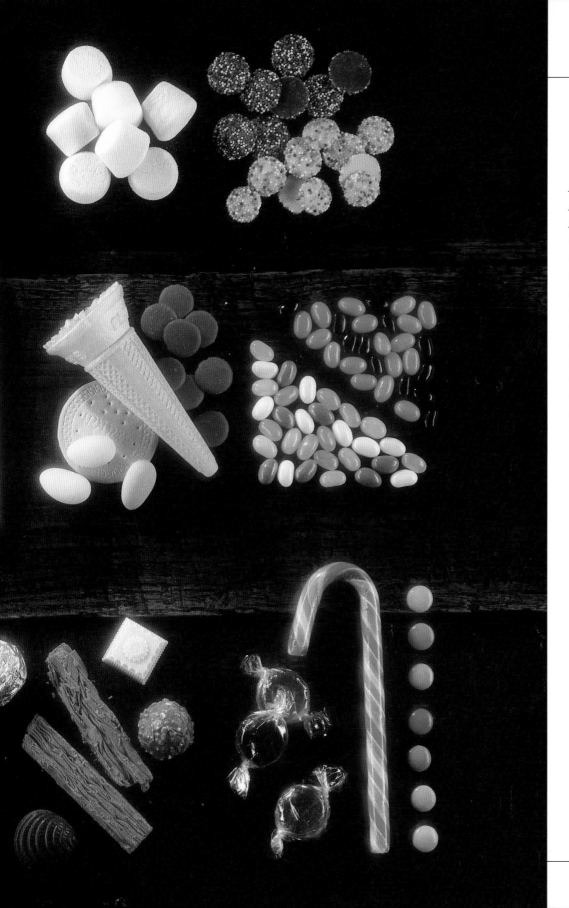

A selection of sweets, chocolates and goodies that are suitable for gingerbread decoration. Just a few of the endless possibilities: foil-wrapped chocolate eggs, marshmallows, non-pareils, flaked almonds, chocolate-covered raisins, striped candy sticks and canes, ice-cream cones (for making trees), biscuits, chocolate buttons, sugared almonds, jelly beans, jellies or gum drops, chocolate bunnies, flaked chocolate, chocolate truffles, boiled sweets and sugar-coated chocolate Smarties or M&Ms.

Basic Equipment

Making and constructing gingerbread is very straightforward and, unlike many other forms of cooking, requires very basic equipment. The most enchanting gingerbread construction is created with imagination and creativity rather than complicated technique. You will have most of the equipment needed for making gingerbread in your kitchen already; for decoration, basic piping and icing equipment will be required. A selection of fancy moulds and cutters will be available in any good kitchenware shops or suppliers.

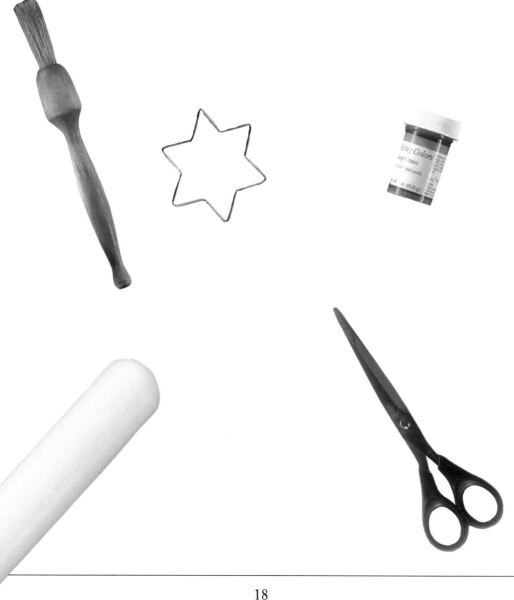

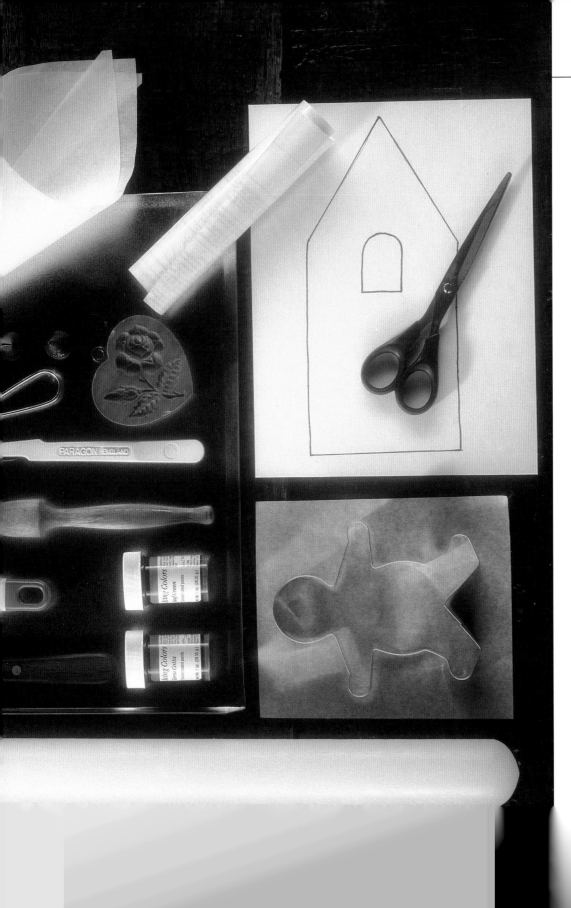

A selection of the items of equipment used in gingerbread making and decorating: rolling pin, cookie or baking sheet, spatula, pizza cutter, sifter or strainer, piping tubes of various sizes and shapes, paper piping bags, a variety of gingerbread and cookie cutters, a range of edible paste food colours, pastry brush, scalpel or craft knife, gingerbread or biscuit moulds, parchment paper, gingerbread men cutters, and thin card or tagboard, scissors and clear contact paper or self-adhesive film templates.

Basic Techniques

About twenty projects are covered in this book, ranging from simple cut-outs and moulded items to grand, lavish constructions. Many things have to be taken into consideration when deciding on a particular project: the amount of time available, the occasion and any special requirements, and your skill level. The following guidelines for preparing and constructing gingerbread apply to all the projects, and basic piping techniques are also covered.

Making and rolling out gingerbread

When making gingerbread you can mix it by hand, like making pastry dough, or in a heavy-duty mixer or food processor. The dough has a smoother texture if mixed in a machine. Before starting work, check to make sure that you have all the ingredients ready in the correct amounts. If you are using templates, make sure these are all ready.

Baking gingerbread

Once you have cut out the gingerbread pieces, it is best to transfer them to a baking or cookie sheet still on their piece of parchment, to avoid distortion of the shaped piece. Place in a preheated oven, according to the recipe, and bake until a light golden brown. When you remove your pieces from the oven they will be soft, but will firm up as they cool.

Once you remove the pieces from the oven, immediately place the template on top of its corresponding piece to make sure the gingerbread has not distorted during baking. If it has distorted, trim it while still warm, in the first few minutes after taking it out of the oven. When cooling your pieces, be sure they are on a flat surface or they will take the shape of the surface on which they are lying.

It is best to leave your gingerbread pieces to set and firm up for about 12–24 hours before assembling them into your chosen project. This will prevent the construction warping and distorting.

In certain climatic conditions, especially where there is a high rainfall or humidity, you will find that gingerbread may go soft while setting. To overcome this problem you will have to bake it slightly longer. Another solution is to rebake softened pieces for 7–10 minutes before assembling them into the chosen project. This will allow them to dry out again and crisp up to the required texture.

Cutting out and adapting templates

All the details, outlines and dimensions for making the templates to construct the gingerbread projects in this book are given with each. For templates that are just made up of straight lines, you might find it easier to follow the measurements and draw up the outlines yourself on to card or tagboard, then cut out the pieces. For rounded shapes, trace the outlines given on to tracing paper and enlarge them if necessary to the required size, either by using a grid system or a photocopier with an enlargement/reduction facility.

The grid method

Trace the design required on a piece of paper, and draw up a light pencil grid over the top of it. On another piece of paper, draw up an area of the size you want the finished image to be, and fill this with the same number of grid squares. Then, copy the original outline square by square on to the second grid. Copy the points at which the original design bisects its grid lines on to the new grid, then follow these marks as a guide for drawing up the new outline. Always check the copied design against the original, and draw over the lines at the end to make sure that they are fluid and continuous.

To make templates more durable, cover them with clear contact paper on both sides. This will prevent grease and flour being absorbed into the board and allow you to wipe the templates clean with a damp cloth, ready to use again.

This book provides instructions and guidance for creating a number of specific gingerbread projects and, it is hoped, inspiration for you to go on to design your own. By bringing

Cutting out gingerbread

1 Once the dough is made (following the recipes on page 15), roll it out on parchment/silicone/baking paper, using a lightly floured rolling pin, to the desired thickness – usually ⅛–¼ in/ 3–6 mm.

3 Lift the template off the dough and remove any excess, leaving the cut-out pieces on the paper. When cutting out your shapes always remember to leave space for expansion during baking.

Using a mould

If you are using a mould, flour it lightly or grease it first. Take a piece of the gingerbread dough and gently press it into the mould, making sure you have filled all the corners well. Gently turn the mould over and tap it to release the shaped dough. Line a baking or cookie sheet with parchment/silicone/baking paper and place the shape on it for baking.

2 Use either cutters or templates to cut out your desired shapes. When using a template, lay it on top of the rolled-out gingerbread dough. Then, using a pizza cutter, sharp palette knife or spatula, trace around the edge of the template, cutting completely through the gingerbread dough.

4 After baking, trim the still-warm gingerbread using the original template as a guide.

together various elements of the template designs in this book, you can construct your very own buildings. Similarly, the gingerbread creations here can be made larger or smaller as required. Adapt the designs accordingly, enlarging or reducing the templates as appropriate.

Choosing and covering a cake board

A very important part of the presentation of a gingerbread construction is the covered board on which it will stand. Cake boards come in an assortment of shapes and sizes and are readily available in most major cake shops. If you cannot find ready-made boards, you can cut your own out of chipboard or marine plywood. Thick tack, poster or photo-mount board will work but make sure it is at least ½ in/1 cm thick.

Bought cake boards are usually already covered in silver or gold paper. But if you want to change the colour, to make sure it complements the scheme chosen for your gingerbread project, for example red at Christmas time, or if you have cut your own board, you will need to cover it yourself. There is, readily available, a whole variety of coloured foils and gift wrapping papers suitable for covering cake boards. Remember when covering your boards that you will just see the edge of the board; as most projects have iced settings which will cover most of the top of the board, 'thumb' lifting room is left clear around the edges.

Assembling your gingerbread project

Of all the preparations suitable for sticking together your gingerbread project, royal icing is the best as it sets quickly and strongly, complements the flavour of the gingerbread, and keeps well. As some people choose to keep their gingerbread projects from year to year as a display piece, this last property is very important. A recipe for royal icing is given on page 15.

To cover a board, place it flat, face down, on the back of the paper. Trim or cut the paper on each side so that the overlap is about 3 in/7.5 cm. Fold over the flaps, working on two opposite sides at a time, and tape them down securely on to the back of the board with sticky tape. Don't worry about 'double folds' at the corners as these won't show if done neatly. For a round board, make snips into the flap all the way round and tape these over individually.

Use a large piping bag with a fair amount of royal icing, and a thin nozzle/tip or tube, to stick the gingerbread pieces together. Remember, when piping royal icing to the edges or trim of the pieces, to use a minimal amount of icing in order to create a strong bond. If too much icing is used, it acts as a lubricant and your pieces will slip and slide against each other and not hold together. Once iced together, hold the pieces in place for about 1 minute for the icing to dry before moving on to the next piece of construction.

Basic piping techniques

These are some of the basic piping techniques used in the projects in this book. They were chosen for their simplicity, and with a minimal amount of practice, any beginner can master them. Advanced decorators will, it is hoped, use these techniques as inspiration for developing their own ideas for decorating gingerbread.

There are a number of metal and plastic piping nozzles/ tips or tubes available on the market. Some people use a syringe or plunger for piping, but with a paper piping bag you have much more control over the pressure and therefore the end result.

~ HOLLY ~

Use a leaf nozzle/tube and pipe a circle of 3 leaves holding the bag at a 45° angle. For the berries, use a small writing tube to pipe a series of 3 dots in the centre, holding the bag at a 90° angle (perpendicular to the surface).

~ SCROLLS ~

Using a small round writing nozzle/tube, hold the bag at a 90° angle and pipe a candy cane-like line with a hook at the end. Pipe another line, with the hook in the opposite direction, to meet it in the centre.

~ HEARTS ~

With a large round nozzle/tube, and holding the bag at a 45° angle, begin to pipe the heart from the top. Pipe one side of the heart, first with a heavy pressure, then as you move down, lessening the pressure into a tail. Stop and pull away. Repeat on the other side.

~ FLOWERS ~

With a medium round nozzle/tube, and holding the bag at a 45° angle, pipe a petal, starting with a heavy pressure and lessening the pressure as you go into the tail. Continue to make 5 petals, joined in the centre to create your flower. With a small round nozzle/tube and the bag at a 90° angle, pipe a single dot in the centre.

~ BOWS ~

With a small round writing nozzle/tube, and holding the bag at a 90° angle, pipe a sideways figure 8. Add 2 streamers coming out from the centre.

~ BASKET-WEAVE ~

Use a serrated-weave or basket-weave nozzle/tube, hold the bag at a 45° angle, and pipe a stripe of icing with a steady even pressure.

~ EMBROIDERED FLOWERS ~

With a small writing nozzle/tube, and holding the bag at a 90° angle, pipe a medium-sized dot for the centre of the flower. Pipe a smaller dot above and below this centre dot. Continue to pipe the rest of the dots in opposite pairs around the larger dot.

~ SPIDERS' WEBS ~

Use a small writing nozzle/tube, hold the bag at a 45° angle, and pipe a star of straight lines working from the centre out. Connect these line with concentric circles of curved lines, each loop curving the same way.

~ STARS ~

Use a medium star nozzle/tube, hold the bag at a 90° angle, and pipe a star with a medium pressure, stopping the pressure before you lift up. When filling-in, pipe the stars close together so no gaps are showing.

~ ZIG-ZAG ~

Use a medium star nozzle/tube, hold the bag at a 45° angle, and pipe a line, squeezing with an even pressure and moving the tube in an up and down motion as you are squeezing.

~ SHELLS ~

Use a star nozzle/tube, hold the bag at a 45° angle, and squeeze with a heavy pressure when piping. Let the icing build up, then lessen the pressure as you pull the bag down to form the tail. Stop and pull away.

~ LATTICE-WORK ~

Use a small round nozzle/tube, hold the bag at a 90° angle, and pipe a series of lines at an angle. Pipe another series of lines in the opposite direction piping over the top of the previous lines.

~ PUMPKINS ~

Use a medium star nozzle/tube, hold the bag at a 90° angle, and squeeze with a heavy pressure to form a star mound. Pipe a stem with a small writing tube.

~ ICICLES ~

Use a large round nozzle/tube. Holding the piping bag at an angle, pipe a sequence of fat lengths where you want the icicles to hang. Squeeze with a heavy pressure and lessen the pressure as you go down into a tail. Break the icicles off to a point after 1 in/2.5 cm or so and pull away.

The main piping techniques used in the projects in this book are (left column, then right): holly wreaths, scrolls, hearts, flowers, bows, basket-weave, embroidered flowers, spiders' webs, stars, fill-in stars, zig-zag, shells, lattice-work, pumpkins and icicles.

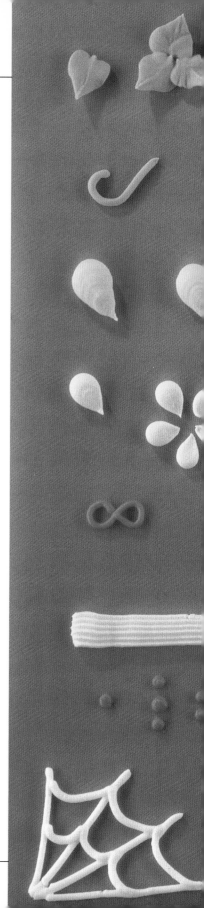

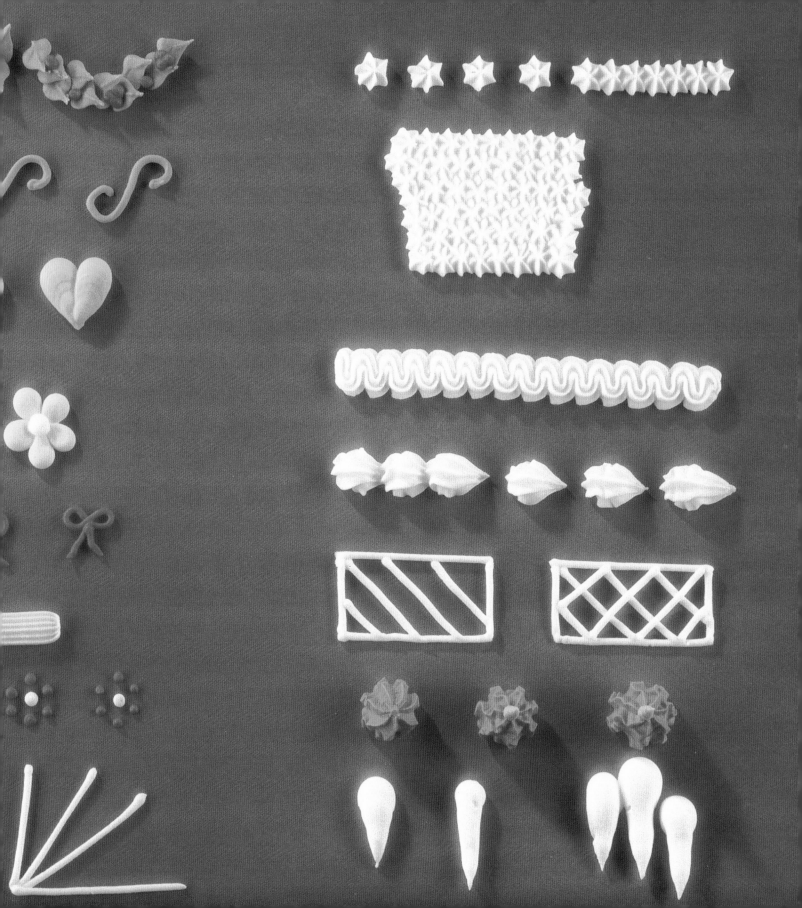

How to pipe trees and bushes

These trees can be prepared months ahead, as they keep very well. Pipe them in moss green icing for a springtime look, or in darker green for a wintery Christmas setting. If you want to stick on candies or sweets, apply them before the icing begins to set and crust over. Or, when dry, you may choose to pipe on decorations.

For bushes, follow the same procedure as for the trees but using marshmallows. When the top of the marshmallow is reached, continue to pipe stars with tails inwards in circles until the centre is filled.

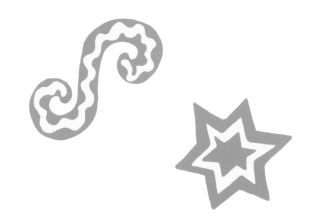

Start with a wax-covered board, to prevent the iced trees from sticking. Upturn a pointed ice-cream cone on to the board, and, using moss green royal icing and a medium star nozzle/tube, pipe a line of stars with tails around the bottom of the cone. Continue in concentric rows, working up the cone to give an 'overhanging' effect, until the top point is reached.

How to pipe lace points

Use a small strip of paper with the lace pattern traced on it and place the pattern under a sheet of wax paper taped down on top of a board. Using a small writing nozzle/tube and royal icing, pipe on top of the wax paper the lace point pattern showing underneath the wax paper. This will allow you to move the pattern around underneath so that you can pipe the whole sheet of wax paper with lace.

How to make windows

There are three basic methods of creating windows for gingerbread buildings. The simplest is to apply parchment paper to the back of the window hole. Rice paper is a possible edible alternative, but tends to dissolve too readily. Sheet gelatine is edible, glass-like and very effective. Both parchment and gelatine are secured with dots of icing to the back of the window hole, and can also be decorated with coloured piping gel for a stained-glass effect. Melting boiled coloured sweets is more complicated, but very effective, creating a glowing glass-like window.

1 To make a stained-glass window using parchment paper or sheet gelatine, first turn the gingerbread piece over. Cut out pieces of paper to a size slightly larger than that of the window hole. Pipe tiny dots of icing around the window and stick the paper piece over, pressing down to secure.

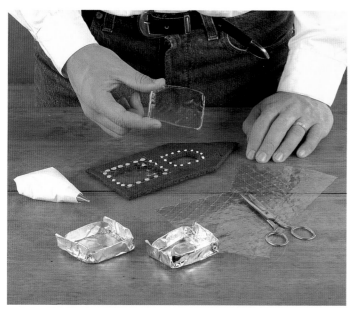

To make a boiled sweet window, first make a square box out of silver foil (simply fold the sides of a square of foil up, crease them and fold back in to make a strong double-thickness side). Put a boiled sweet or candy inside and place in an oven preheated to 240°F/170°C/gas 3 for approximately 5–7 minutes until the sweet has melted completely and filled the box. Remove from the oven and allow to cool completely. Once cooled, peel off the foil and attach the window pane to the back of the window area with dots of royal icing.

2 Turn the gingerbread piece over so that the face is uppermost. Mix a palette of coloured piping gels, applying the colour paste to each gel gradually to ensure the exact shade required is reached. The coloured gels can go into individual paper piping bags (unless you feel confident enough to apply them directly with a thin implement). Pipe tiny areas of the coloured gels into the windows, covering all the parchment or sheet gelatine.

Gingerbread Cut-Outs and Simple Shapes

'Hot spice-gingerbread, hot! hot! all hot!
Come buy my spice-gingerbread, smoking hot!'
TRADITIONAL STREET CRY

The cutting out and baking of shapes from gingerbread is one of the most traditional and popular ways in which this sweet paste is used. Gingerbread men were first seen on sale in the streets of London in the 1600s, with a cut-out character called 'Johnny Boy', whose legs were supposed to be so springy that he once jumped out of the oven and escaped. Other popular cut-outs were sheep, dogs, hearts and flowers. By the late 1800s street hawkers on both sides of the Atlantic were selling factory-produced gingerbread ducks, lambs, roosters, lords and ladies. There was even a gingerbread reproduction of King George riding on horseback. Cut-outs are one of the most accessible methods of using gingerbread for children and beginners. Special metal cut-outs are readily available, but it is easy enough to make your own card templates and cut around these to make men, girls, hearts, stars, moons, Christmas trees, and even apples and pineapples. By using a variety of gingerbread recipes, you can produce a mixture of light- and dark-coloured gingerbread cut-outs, to great effect.

Gingerbread cut-outs can be used in many different ways. By making a hole at the top they can be strung with ribbon and hung as cookie ornaments on Christmas trees and festive wreaths, or as little name tags. They can make amusing place marks at a tea table. Cut-out trees and people often form two-dimensional additions to a gingerbread house presentation; another lovely idea is to hide miniature gingerbread men inside the building.

OPPOSITE: *Simple gingerbread men and heart shapes, decorated in a variety of ways with white piped icing, can be attached with ribbons to make beautiful festive wreaths. The gingerbread used for these is a traditional rich, dark mixture (see recipe 2 on page 15).*

Gingerbread Cut-Outs

If you are just beginning to work with gingerbread, start with a simple project like these cut-outs. When creating these you will learn all the basics needed for constructing the other, more complex, projects in the book. They are also a perfect way to practise your decorating skills.

Gingerbread men are decorated here, but you may use any cookie cutters you wish. There are literally thousands avail-able throughout the world and they can be purchased at most specialist bakeware shops or grocery stores.

1 × quantity of gingerbread (recipe 1, page 15) when rolled out will be enough for approximately 12–24 cut-outs, depending on the size of the cutter; for example, about 15–18 medium-sized gingerbread men. Recipe 2 makes 3 × this amount.

1 With a rolling pin, roll the gingerbread dough out on parchment paper to a thickness of about ⅛ in/3 mm. For easier release, dip your cookie cutter lightly in flour before pressing it into the rolled-out dough. Gently press the cutter directly down, allowing it to sink into the dough. Press on all edges to make sure that all of the cutter has cut through the dough.

2 Remove excess dough around the shape by lifting it directly up and off the parchment paper. This excess dough can be saved and re-rolled one more time.

3 If these cut-out shapes are to have ribbon strung through them they will need to have a hole inserted. Using a drinking straw or metal tube, press a hole at the top of the shape.

4 Raisins, sweets and other goodies may be added once the shapes have been cut out. If they are placed on before baking, they will actually bake into the shaped gingerbread.

5 The cut-outs may be decorated with a variety of coloured royal icing using the techniques shown on page 25.

Decorative possibilities for gingerbread men are limitless. They can be simply adorned with raisins for eyes and buttons, in traditional style; decorated with plain white icing for a folksy effect; made to resemble characters such as Santa Claus or have various items of clothing such as waistcoats and scarves piped in bright colours. Individual names could be piped on for children.

Each item can be decorated individually: the classic white piped royal icing creates a wonderfully traditional, nostalgic effect, or coloured icing or frosting can be used. Sweets and candies stuck on with a little icing are used for eyes, buttons, or jewels.

Christmas Ornaments and Window Hangings

Many stories are told of how tight money was, especially at Christmas, during the great Depression of the 1920s. One story I remember in particular was of some people not having money to decorate their homes or their Christmas trees, so they resorted to hand-made food items.

This household hand-strung their garlands with a needle and thread, using popcorn and fresh cranberries, alternating them as they went along. For the tree decorations, the mother baked gingerbread men with raisin eyes, noses and buttons. They were then festively hung on the tree, using scraps of coloured ribbon or yarn.

Here I have used Christmas cookie cutters and decorated them with Christmas colours. There are thousands of suitably shaped cookie cutters, so use what suits you best. The ornaments need not just be used on the tree, but can be strung with longer ribbons and hung in windows as window hangings. One recipe quantity (page 15) will be sufficient for about 25 cut-out ornaments, depending on the sizes of cutters used.

Moulded Gingerbread Shapes

Antique moulds, dating back many centuries, amply demonstrate the long history of the technique of moulding cookies. Today, both commercial companies and individuals are producing such moulds. Some of the moulds created are hand-made reproductions of antique specimens, showing exquisite details; others are modern-day designs with simple details.

Moulds are available in most specialist bakeware shops and come in a large variety of sizes and designs suitable for all occasions. You may even stumble across a mould at an antique shop or flea market.

1 × quantity of gingerbread (recipe 1, page 15) will be enough for approximately 12–18 medium-sized moulds.

1 Moulds are available in hundreds of shapes and sizes throughout the world. Although the materials used to produce them are all quite different, the procedure of moulding gingerbread is usually the same. Begin by dusting the moulds lightly with flour to ensure easy release of the dough from the mould.

2 With your hand, firmly press the gingerbread dough into the mould, making sure all areas have been filled. The dough will have a thickness of about ¼–½ in/½–1 cm, depending on the mould used.

Moulded gingerbread tends to be thicker because of the need to get a good impression from the mould.

3 Trim any excess dough that has extended over the edge of the mould by cutting it off with a spatula. Use the edge of the mould as a guide to get the edge even.

4 Tap the mould lightly in the hand or on a work surface to release the dough from the mould. Place it on a baking sheet lined with parchment paper. Bake in an oven preheated to 350°F/180°C/gas 4 for 24–25 minutes, until golden brown. *Note*: If light- and dark-coloured doughs are going to be used together press the 'accent' colour into the impressions in which they are required and add the background colour on top.

A huge variety of gingerbread, biscuit and cookie moulds are available, from genuine antique examples to modern reproductions and contemporary designs. They can be left plain or simply edged with white piping.

Holly Wreath

Ready to greet visiting guests at Christmas this gingerbread holly wreath will add a warm, cosy feeling to any household. Constructed of decorated cut-outs, this wreath is very simple to create.

The holly cut-outs may be replaced with hearts to construct a St. Valentine's Day wreath, or even simple cut-out flowers for an everyday wreath. With the large variety of cookie cutters available on the market, it is possible to design a wreath for any occasion.

REQUIREMENTS
gingerbread holly cut-outs made with
$1/2$ × *quantity of recipe 2 (page 15)*
cardboard circle
$2^1/2$ *cups/1lb/450g royal icing:*
2 cups/$^3/4$lb/350g moss green
$^1/2$ *cup/$^1/4$lb/100g red*
$1^1/2$ *yards /$1^1/2$ metres of red ribbon*
wire coat-hanger (for the back)

The completed wreath is extremely effective with its strong, sculptural shapes and two-colour piping in Christmassy shades of bright red and leaf green. It could be hung on a door or above a fireplace, perhaps opposite a mirror. If kept out of the way of accidental brushes and knocks, the wreath will last throughout the festive season and beyond.

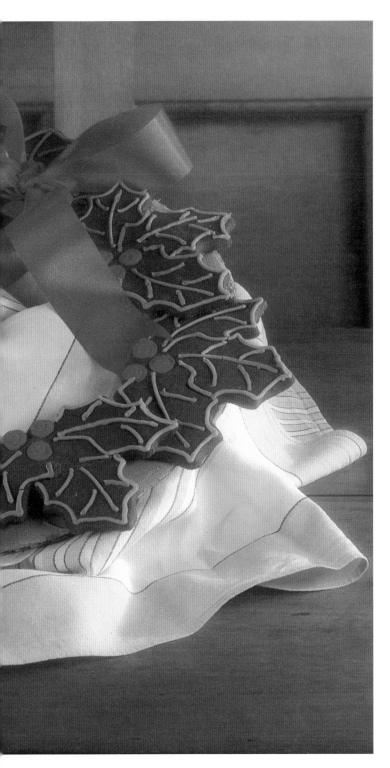

1 Cut out card templates to the dimensions required, and make the gingerbread pieces. You will need 8 holly leaves (cut out with a holly cutter), and a cardboard circle with a 3 in/7.5 cm frame and outside diameter of 12 in/30 cm, for the wreath (see page 39 for the outline, and page 20 for how to trace and make card templates).

2 Decorate the holly and berry cut-outs before applying them to the cardboard circle base. To do so, use coloured royal icing and a writing tube to outline all the inside detail lines and edges of the cut-outs.

3 Ice the cardboard circle underneath with a thin layer of royal icing coloured the same shade of green as the cut-outs. Once that is iced and dry, apply the decorated cut-outs with dabs of green royal icing piped on their backs or on the base. Arrange them so that they divide the circle into quarters, and press them directly on.

4 Pipe large dabs of green royal icing in the centre of the open spaces remaining on the cardboard circle. Place the remaining 4 cut-outs on the dabs of icing, making sure that they adhere to it. If they do not you may need to pipe a larger blob. The edges of these last 4 cut-outs will overlap those of the first 4 to give a more 3-dimensional effect.

5 Once all 8 cut-outs have been added, tie a double-looped bow of 1 in/2.5 cm red ribbon with streamers coming down from it. Locate the hook hanger on the back of the circle to indicate the top of the wreath and pipe a dab of green royal icing on the front of the wreath at the same point. Press the centre of the bow on the blob of icing. Allow all the icing to dry with the wreath flat for 24 hours before lifting.

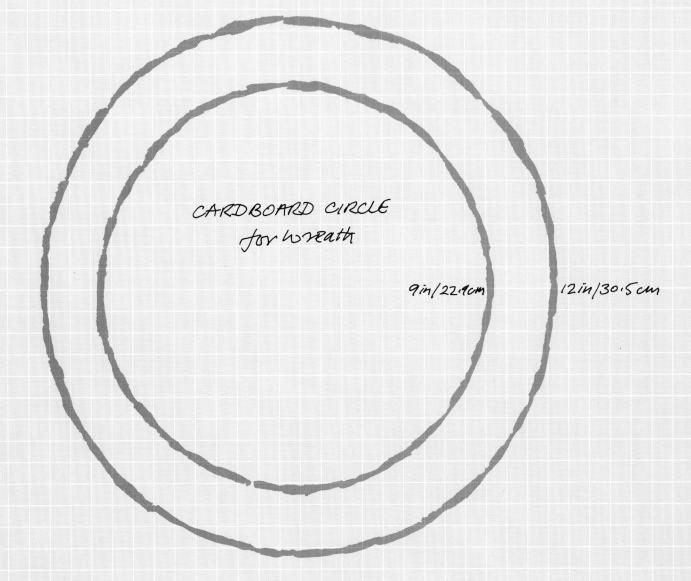

CARDBOARD CIRCLE
for wreath

9in/22.9cm   12in/30.5cm

Simple Gingerbread Buildings

'An I had but one penny in the world, thou should'st have it to buy gingerbread.'
WILLIAM SHAKESPEARE Loves Labours Lost

The tradition of making houses from gingerbread originates from where the constructions are called Knusperhäuschen *('snack-' or 'nibble-houses'),* Hexenhäusle *('witch's house'), or plain* Lebkuchenhäusle *('gingerbread house'). This craft has spread through the world, and has become closely associated with the celebration of the biggest festivals of the year. A wonderful gingerbread house makes a fine centrepiece for any festive occasion, and can either be dismantled and eaten, or preserved for display. Of course the suitability of a gingerbread construction for any event derives principally from the decorative detailing you apply, so I have given variations and seasonal alternatives for additional inspiration.*

Cut-outs and shapes are enormous fun, but the building of houses and cottages is one of the real pinnacles of the gingerbread-maker's art. Once you have developed the basic skills you will want to experiment with architecture – and the techniques are deliciously simple. The basic structures described in this chapter will set you on your way, and give you the inspiration to adapt the shapes into more complex house ideas of your own (perhaps a gingerbread version of a friend's home, which makes a delightful hostess gift).

OPPOSITE: *Gingerbread constructions don't have to be the classic 'Hansel and Gretel' candy-covered cottage. The basic building components and techniques of construction can be adapted for many other creations, by just adjusting the proportions of the walls and roof, and by adding extensions, porches, gables, and steeples (as in this country church).*

A Woodland Cottage

This simple cottage has an unusual A-line structure and an appealing 'fairy tale' look to it. It is fairly straightforward to construct, with its flat front and back, and two-slab roof. It has a somewhat folksy, alpine air to it, and so I present it as 'a woodman's cottage'. In this project a wintery style and setting is shown; other equally attractive versions include the Scandinavian-style spring cottage on page 46.

other equally attractive versions include the Scandinavian-style spring cottage on page 46.

REQUIREMENTS

gingerbread pieces made with
1 × quantity of recipe 2 (page 15)
12 in/30 cm square board, covered in red foil paper
5 cups/2¼lb/1kg royal icing:
3½ cups/1½lb/675g white
½ cup/¼lb/100g red
1 cup/½lb/225g green
stripy coloured mints or candies
coffee sugar crystals (for the pathway)
2 ice-cream cones (for the trees)
2 marshmallows (for the bushes)
1 chocolate flake (for the woodpile)

The finished gingerbread house is charming in its simplicity and would make a lovely centrepiece at winter and Christmas festivities. A more effective, and traditional, result can often be achieved by a careful contrast of colour, and by avoiding too many multi-coloured sweets and candies.

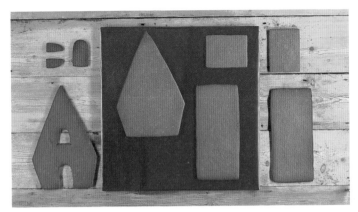

1 Cut out card templates to the dimensions required. You will need 2 front and back pieces, identical except for the cut-out arched door and window on one; 2 small rectangle pieces for the wall sides; 2 long rectangles for the roof, a small arch shape for the door and a slightly smaller arch cut in half for the shutters (see page 47 for the outlines, and page 20 for how to trace and make card templates).

Roll out your gingerbread to a thickness of about ¼ in/6 mm on a lightly greased surface. Bake (in batches as necessary) in an oven preheated to 350°F/ 180°C/gas 4 for 10–12 minutes, until crisp and coloured. Then trim to neaten and cool on a wire rack.

2 Begin to construct the house, using royal icing as glue. First, pipe icing along the bottom edge of the gingerbread back, and secure it upright near the back of the board, at a slight angle.

Then, pipe 3 lower sides of one of the wall sides, and carefully join it at right angles to the back piece. As icing dries so quickly, it is piped on the edges directly before you join them.

3 Pipe icing on the bottom edges of the gingerbread front, and on the right-hand lower side. Secure it on the board so that it juts up neatly against the side wall, and is parallel to the back piece. Then, pipe the 3 lower sides of the remaining side wall and fit it snugly into place to complete the basic structure.

4 Place on the roof slabs. First pipe heavily along the edges of the house structure on one side, the 2 roof lines, and the top of the side wall. Place a roof piece on carefully so that it fits exactly at the top of the house – it will overhang a little at the bottom (and at the front and back) to make the eaves. Fill in any unevenness or gaps underneath with icing to secure thoroughly. Repeat with the other side.

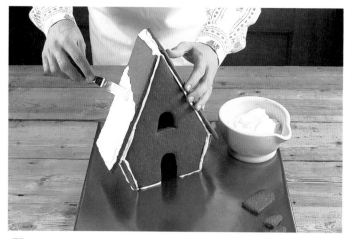

5 Now decorate the roof, working on one side at a time as the icing will dry out quickly. Spread royal icing all over the roof with a spatula, roughly peaking it to resemble snow. Next stick on your unwrapped sweets or candies, pushing them in gently and arranging them in a random but fairly balanced pattern.

6 When you have finished securing the sweets on the roof, you can tidy up all the joins with a line of tight scroll piping. First pipe along the front eaves with a thick line, then around the door and window with a slightly thinner line, along the base and outside edges of the house, and all around the eaves and along the top ridge of the roof.

7 Pipe a thin decorative line around the 2 shutters and the door, adding a small door handle at the same time. With a blob of royal icing, secure the shutters flat on the front of the house on either side of the window. Then attach the door on one side so that it appears to be slightly open.

8 Decorative details can now be piped on the house facade with coloured royal icing – red and green are used here for a wintery, Christmas effect. A wreath is shell-piped over the window, then a red thread bow and berries. A smaller wreath is piped on the door. On the shutters and at the 'window box' are piped holly leaves and berries. Red scroll lines are piped on either side of the facade, and red hearts add a finishing touch.

9 The setting is now created – here, a winter snow scene. Spread royal icing all over the board so that it juts up against the house on all sides, using a spatula to create a peaked snow effect.

10 Add a curving pathway of sprinkled coloured coffee crystals; shades of brown are particularly appropriate. Add trees and bushes (see page 26 for techniques) and cut up chocolate logs to make a little woodpile by the doorway.

11 Finish off by piping icicles on the eaves of the house with white royal icing. Hold the piping bag underneath the roof to achieve the right angle and to avoid breaking off the hanging pieces, and pipe a sequence of fat lengths down from the eaves, breaking them off to a point after 1 in/2.5 cm or so. If you like, you can then sift a little caster or superfine sugar over the whole scene for a shimmery effect.

This alternatively decorated version also has a woodland setting, but has a Scandinavian spring or summer theme. Follow the step-by-step instructions given above for the construction of the house, but then cover the roof and pipe the joins with brown icing, and use chocolate truffles, buttons and chocolate-covered nuts in shades of cream and brown to decorate the roof. The piping on the facade varies slightly and flowers are shown at the window rather than holly. The board is covered with green icing, peaked heavily for grass, and little piped flowers are also added.

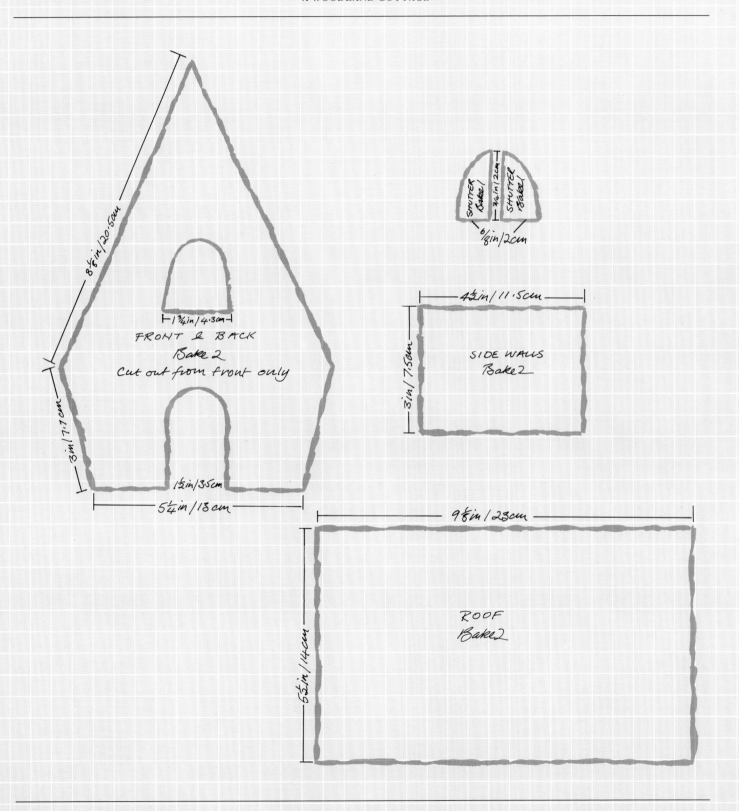

8½ in/20·5cm

1¾ in/4·3cm

FRONT & BACK
Bake 2
Cut out from front only

3 in/7·7 cm

1½ in/3·5cm

5¼ in/13cm

SHUTTER
Bake 1

SHUTTER
Bake 1

¾ in/2cm

6½ in/2cm

4½ in/11·5cm

SIDE WALLS
Bake 2

3 in/7·5cm

9⅛ in/23cm

ROOF
Bake 2

5½ in/14cm

Christmas House

This house, with its Christmas theme, is a very basic building for anyone to construct. The effectiveness is all due to the decoration. You may choose to scale the pattern down in size in order to build a number of houses. In this way you could create your own enchanting village, perhaps with a baker's shop, grocery store, etc.

An alternative Easter theme has been created to demonstrate that this project need not only be constructed at Christmas. By changing the snow in the yard to grass, along with the overall decorations and colour theme, you can design a house for any time of the year.

REQUIREMENTS
gingerbread pieces made with
1 × quantity of recipe 2 (page 15)
12 × 15 in/30 × 37.5 cm board,
covered with green foil paper
7½ cups/3¼lb/1.45kg royal icing:
4 cups/1¾lb/750g white
2 cups/¾lb/350g forest green
1 cup/½lb/225g brown
½ cup/¼lb/100g red
sheet gelatine (for the windows)
1 marshmallow (for the bush)
12oz/350g non-pareils (for the roof)
1 tube red Smarties or M&Ms
(for the pathway and the roof)
1 ice-cream cone (for the tree)

The finished house has been put in a wintery setting by adding fir trees and bushes on the snow; decorate the former with piped red baubles to give the appearance of an outside Christmas tree. A limited colour palette of brown, red, green and white creates an authentic festive and seasonal feel.

1 Cut out card templates to the dimensions required, and make the gingerbread pieces. You will need 2 front and back rectangles, one plain and one with a cut-out door and double-window; 2 identical pointed side pieces with 2 windows each; 2 long rectangles for the roof; 1 small door, and smaller window-shutter rectangles (allow plenty for breakages). See page 51 for the outlines, and page 20 for how to trace and make card templates.

2 To start this Christmas House you'll need to apply sheet gelatine to the backs of the walls where windows have been cut out. See page 27 for techniques. Pipe a line of royal icing along the bottom edge of the back wall and place it off centre on the board, slightly towards the back. Take a pointed side wall, pipe a line of icing along the bottom and sides and place it against the back wall. On the opposite end repeat the same procedure with the other pointed side wall.

The front wall can now be added by piping a line of royal icing along the bottom edge and butting it up against the 2 side walls.

With all 4 walls now standing, pipe a line of icing around all the top edges. Place the 2 roof pieces directly on the iced edges. All 10 shutters are now added by placing a small dot of icing behind each piece and then positioning one of them on either side of each window. Pipe the window and shutter trims with a shell border.

3 Add the door by piping a line of icing along the left-hand side and attaching it to the left-hand side of the door opening. You may then add a shell border trim along the top and side of the door.

Using brown royal icing, pipe a series of dots along the bottom edge of the roof spacing them far enough apart to fit a non-pareil on each dot. This will stick them individually to the roof. For the second row, pipe the dots alternately in between the non-pareils already in place so that the rows will fit snugly.

Another alternative is to pipe a dot of icing on the back of each non-pareil then place it on the roof instead of piping a continuous line of dots, to be sure the sweets will fit.

4 Starting with the side wall, pipe a thick zig-zag border along the wall seams and roof edges. Finish by piping a line along the top of the roof.

5 Using the spatula at an angle, spread a thin layer of royal icing along the front and sides of the house. When spreading the 'snow' use a sharp swirling motion to create the effect of drifts. Before the icing begins to set, scatter your chosen candies for the pathway, leading out from the door to the edge of the snow.

Pipe garlands of holly under the eaves, clusters of holly on each shutter and a wreath on the door (see page 23 for techniques). Pipe icicles hanging down from the roof on both the front and back and all the edges of the house. Finally, add a row of red sweets along the roof top ridge, and a tree and shrub on the snow-filled yard.

To create this alternative Easter House, construct the building in exactly the same way as described in the steps above, but cover your board in a paler shade of paper, and pipe the edges of the construction and the roof with pale yellow icing. Sugared almonds are used on the roof, and striped lollipops or suckers in pastel shades have been secured on to the sides. Instead of piping holly wreaths on the shutters and under the eaves, pipe simple scrolls and folk hearts in complementary colours. Pale green icing has been used for grass and also to cover the tree and bush, so that they seem to have a new spring growth of leaves. A miniature chocolate Easter bunny stands outside.

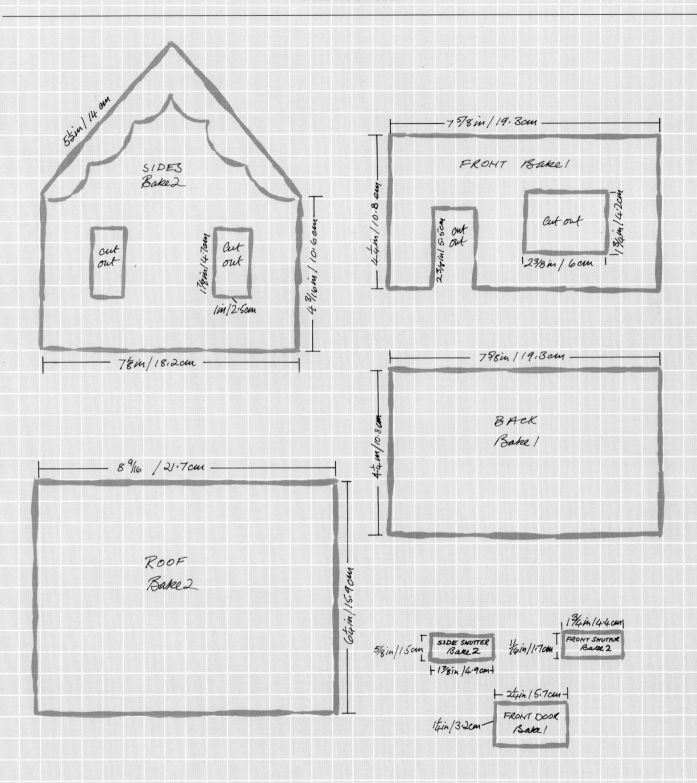

SIDES
Bake 2

5½in / 14 cm

cut out

cut out

1⅞in / 4.7cm

1in / 2.5cm

4³/₁₆in / 10.6cm

7⅛in / 18.2cm

FRONT Bake 1

7⅝in / 19.30cm

4¼in / 10.8 cm

cut out

2³/₈in 5.5cm

cut out

2³/₈in / 6cm

1¾in / 4.2cm

BACK
Bake 1

7⅝in / 19.3cm

4¼in / 10.8cm

ROOF
Bake 2

8⁹/₁₆ / 21.7cm

6¼in / 15.9cm

SIDE SHUTTER
Bake 2

5/8in / 1.5cm

1³/₈in / 4.9cm

FRONT SHUTTER
Bake 2

1¾in / 4.4cm

1/16in / 1.7cm

FRONT DOOR
Bake 1

2¼in / 5.7cm

1¼in / 3.2cm

Hansel and Gretel House

'Suddenly Hansel and Gretel came into a clearing in the forest and saw a cottage with a steep roof that reached almost to the ground. When they went close up to it they saw that the cottage was made of gingerbread biscuits and was decorated with festive coloured candies, cookies and icing.'

Inspired by this passage from the fairy tale of Hansel and Gretel, this enchanting but simply shaped cottage with its bright colours will delight children of all ages. The basic construction is very simple, and so can easily be adapted for other occasions, such as the Christmas Cottage shown. It is a fairy tale house, so use your imagination when decorating it.

This sweet-covered gingerbread house is every child's dream – the classic fairy tale Hansel and Gretel house come true. This version is quite traditional and simple; you could take the decoration a stage further, however, and completely encrust the walls with different-coloured sweets and candies. Perhaps a cut-out gingerbread witch should also be added, for authenticity . . .

REQUIREMENTS

gingerbread pieces made with

2 × quantity of recipe 1 (page 15)

14 in/35 cm square board, covered with gold foil paper

8½ cups/3lb 10oz/1.575kg royal icing:

4½ cups/1lb 14oz/800g moss green

2 cups/¾lb/350g white

1 cup/½lb/225g brown

½ cup/¼lb/100g red

¼ cup/2oz/50g yellow

¼ cup/2oz/50g pink

sheet gelatine (for the window)

32 round tea biscuits

1 tube of Smarties or M&Ms

2 striped candy sticks or canes

1 boiled sweet or sucker (for the front decoration)

6 red jellies or gum drops (for the roof)

8 oz/225g boiled sweets (for the pathway)

2 ice-cream cones (for the trees)

4 marshmallows (for the bushes)

2 gingerbread men

2 Apply sheet gelatine to the back of the window on the front wall as shown on page 27. Pipe a line of royal icing along the bottom of the back wall of the house. Position on the board. Take 1 side wall and run a line of icing along the 2 sides and the bottom edge and butt the piece up against the back wall. Repeat this for the other side wall, then fix on the front piece. Pipe a line of icing along the top edge of all the walls and fix on 1 roof piece, then the other.

1 Cut out card templates to the dimensions required, and make the gingerbread pieces. You will need 2 pointed front and back pieces, one plain and one with a cut-out door and window; 2 identical plain rectangular side pieces; 2 long rectangles for the roof; 1 door; 2 small window-shutters if required and 2 cut-out people (see page 55 for the outlines, and page 20 for how to trace and make card templates).

3 Pipe a zig-zag of brown royal icing around the window, door and side walls. Next, dab royal icing on the back of the biscuits and position them on the roof, like tiles. Fix a Smartie or M&M in the centre of each biscuit, with a dab of royal icing on the back to make it adhere. Pipe a line of red royal icing around the edge of every biscuit.

4 Pipe a white zig-zag border around the roof edges and stick the candy canes upright to the side trims. Secure the boiled sweet or sucker to the front wall, and enhance with yellow icing swirls. Place gum drops along the top seam of the roof. Fix the door on the front wall with a series of dots piped in royal icing, and pipe a white edge around it. Fix the shutters to both sides of the window and decorate the edges with red piping and pink flowers. Pipe white hearts on the side walls for decoration, and red hearts and white lines under the eaves.

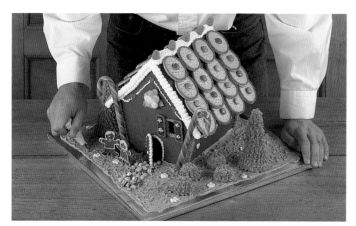

5 Using a spatula, spread a thin layer of green icing over the top of the cake board for the grass. With your spatula, pat up and down on the fresh icing to lift it into peaks. While the icing is still fresh, press your pathway candies into the grass. Pipe trees and bushes (see page 26 for techniques), and position the outlined Hansel and Gretel figures where you want them. Pipe flowers throughout the yard.

This sumptuous variation of the gingerbread house follows the same construction method as that of the Hansel and Gretel building, but is transformed by its decoration. A sophisticated selection of chocolate truffles has been used, to create a more grown-up effect.

Build the house as described in the steps above, then pipe white icing all over the roof, and thick zig-zag lines along all the wall seams. Cover the roof with rich truffles and chocolate buttons, and place a row of Maltesers or Chocolate Kisses along the top ridge; icicles are piped around the eaves of the roof. The shutters are piped over in white, and have red decorative piped scrolls. Holly wreaths in red and green decorate the walls and door, as do red hearts and white scrolls; a trail of holly winds around the doorway. The snow-covered garden has a pathway of milk- and white-chocolate buttons, a woodpile of flaked chocolate and forest green-coloured bushes and fir trees. Make a small snowman out of white fondant/sugarpaste to complete the scene.

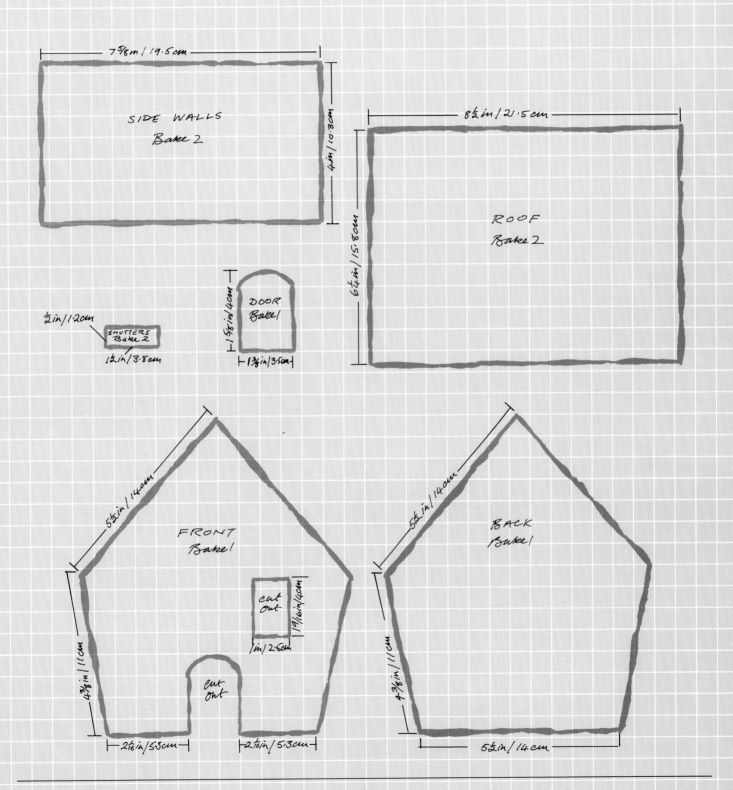

SIDE WALLS
Bake 2

7 5/8 in / 19.5 cm

4 in / 10.3 cm

ROOF
Bake 2

8 1/2 in / 21.5 cm

6 1/4 in / 15.8 cm

SHUTTERS
Bake 2

1/2 in / 1.2 cm

1 1/2 in / 3.8 cm

DOOR
Bake 1

1 5/8 in / 4 cm

1 3/8 in / 3.5 cm

FRONT
Bake 1

5 1/2 in / 14 cm

cut
Out

1 9/16 in / 4 cm

1 in / 2.5 cm

4 3/8 in / 11 cm

cut
Out

2 1/8 in / 5.5 cm

2 1/16 in / 5.3 cm

BACK
Bake 1

5 1/2 in / 14 cm

4 3/8 in / 11 cm

5 1/2 in / 14 cm

Country Church

Churches have called people together for worship and community gatherings for centuries. In the part of the world in which I live, it is common, when driving in the rural countryside, to come across a small white country church with its tall steeple, set all alone with perhaps a grove of trees growing beside it. It was from such scenes that the idea of a simple gingerbread church came about.

This country church is decorated with a winter scene, appropriate for a Christmas centrepiece. Alternatively, a spring church is a wonderful idea for an Easter centrepiece. A church could also be included as one of the buildings in a gingerbread village.

This rural church has a sweet and simple appearance; the setting is a wintertime one, with the snow on the ground remaining but beginning to thaw from the church roof. A few icicles survive on the eaves and trees. The stained-glass windows are particularly effective; coloured piping gel has been used on parchment paper, although for complete edibility, rice paper or sheet gelatine can be used.

gingerbread pieces made with
1 × quantity of recipe 2 (page 15)
12 × 15 in/30 × 37.5 cm board, covered with foil paper
8¼ cups/3½lb/1.55kg royal icing:
4 cups/1lb 14oz/750g white
2½/1lb/450g brown
1½ cups/10oz/300g moss green
¼ cup/2oz/50g red
sheet gelatine (for the windows)
parchment paper (for the windows)
10 tbsp piping gel (for the windows):
2 tbsp each in 5 colours
2 ice-cream cones (for the steeple and the tree)
1 cup/8oz/225g crystallized sugar (for the pathway)
1 marshmallow (for the bush)

2 You will need the 3 pieces of the church which have windows cut out of them (the front and 2 side walls), along with a blank back wall and the two pieces for the sloping roof. Cut pieces of paper just larger than the cut-out window spaces, and secure them to the back of the gingerbread cut-outs with dots of icing. In this case, instead of an edible product, like sheet gelatine or boiled candies (see page 27), I chose to use parchment paper for these church windows because the effect is much bolder when the coloured piping gel is applied.

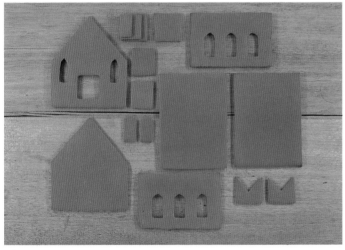

1 Cut out card templates to the dimensions required, and make the gingerbread pieces. You will need 2 pointed front and back pieces, one plain and one with a cut-out door and 2 thin windows; 2 identical long rectangular side pieces with 3 arched windows; 2 large rectangles for the roof; 3 various-sized squares and 2 'zig-zag' pieces for the steeple; 2 door pieces and also 3 small slabs for the steps (see page 61 for the outlines, and page 20 for how to trace and make card templates).

3 Using paste food colours, tint the piping gel to the colours desired. Piping gel is tinted by adding a small amount of paste food colouring a little at a time. Once the gel is coloured you'll need to put each colour in a separate parchment bag using a small round tip. Turn the walls over and pipe zig-zag spots of alternate colours on the parchment in the windows to achieve a stained-glass effect. Allow to dry.

Using white royal icing and a round tip, pipe a line of dots around the trim of each window to finish them off.

4 On the blank back wall of the church pipe a medium line of royal icing along the bottom edge and place it on the board. I chose to angle the church slightly and set it towards the back of the board to allow for more 'front yard'. Have a jar or glass handy to rest the piece against until it sets in position. Next pipe a medium line of icing on the inner edge of the back wall and on the bottom edge of both side walls. Place the side walls on the board, butting them up against the back wall. Once the side walls are standing, pipe a medium line of icing along their front edges and add the front wall, butting it up against the side walls.

Pipe a medium line of icing along the top edges of all 4 walls, and place the 2 roof pieces on top of the iced edges, one at a time.

5 To add the steps, take the largest of the 3 squares, pipe a dot of royal icing on its underside and place it on the board against the front wall, aligned with the doorway. Add the second and third steps in the same way.

The steeple base is added to the roof by piping a thin line of icing along 1 'zig-zag' piece in which the bottom 'V' has been cut out. Place it on the roof, one-third from the front of the church. Next add the 2 square sides by piping a line of icing along the 2 sides and bottom of each piece and placing them alongside the front piece already added, so that they are a little way down the slope. The back piece is then added by piping a line of icing along the bottom cut-out 'V' and positioning it on the roof.

6 The top lid to the steeple is then added by piping a line of icing completely around the top edges and placing the smaller square directly on top. An ice-cream cone is then added, by piping a line of icing around its rim, turning it upside down and gently pressing it into place.

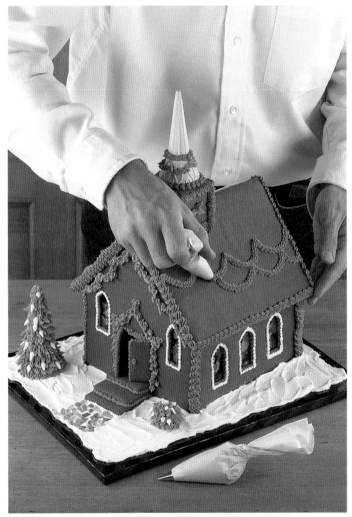

7 With a spatula, spread a thin layer of white royal icing on the board to represent a snowy yard. Do not spread the icing all the way to the edge of the board, so as to allow 'thumb room' to pick it up. Now add the pathway by scattering brown crystallized sugar pieces in a wide swathe.

Using brown royal icing, trim the doors, steps, seams of the church and steeple edges of the roof using dot and zig-zag borders. Moss green holly garlands and red bows are piped along the eaves and around the door and steeple. A tree and bush with icicles are then added to the yard (see page 26 for techniques).

Next, pipe scallops over the slopes of the roof, starting half-way down and dividing each side of the roof horizontally in 4. Use the zig-zag technique.

8 The top half of the roof has been left bare so that we can spread a layer of snow on it. Using a spatula, spread a thin layer of royal icing on this empty part of the roof. Using a swirling motion with the end of the spatula creates a drifted effect on the snow.

Finally, pipe icicles coming down from the roof and steeple edges (see page 24 for techniques).

A variation in decoration – this church has a much more puritanical air. In a summer setting of green grass and piped flowers, the ornamentation is completely two-tone, with white icing on brown gingerbread. Follow the construction methods outlined in the steps above, but pipe white zig-zag lines along the seams, in scalloped lines all over the roof, with double-borders around the windows, and simple scrolls on the steeple. A cross has been piped on to the front of the church. The only splash of colour is the bright stained-glass windows; primary colours have been used for maximum impact.

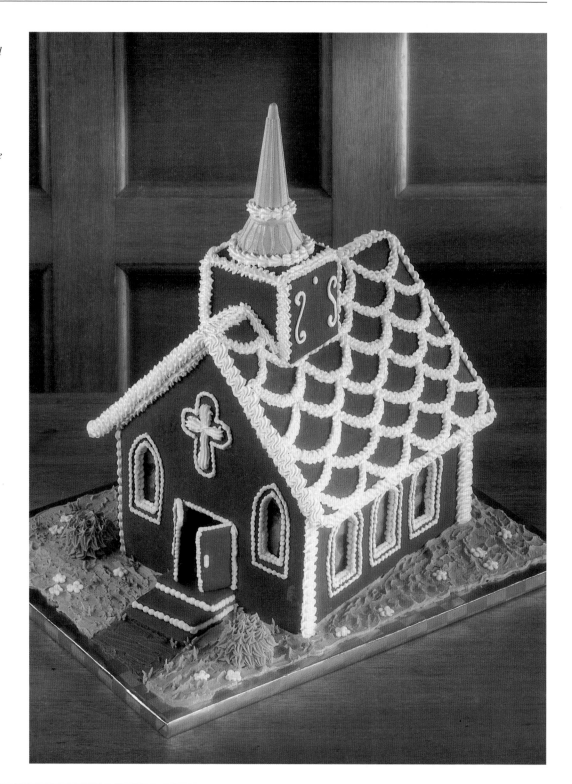

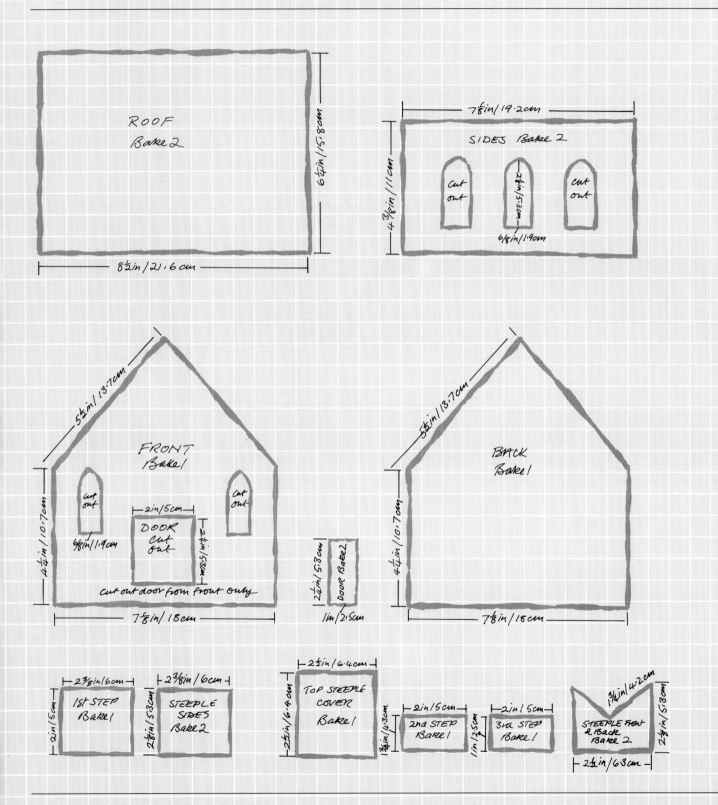

ROOF
Bake 2

6¼in / 15.8cm

8½in / 21.6cm

SIDES Bake 2

7⅝in / 19.2cm

4⅜in / 11cm

Cut out

2⅛in / 5.3cm

Cut out

¾in / 1.9cm

FRONT
Bake 1

5½in / 13.7cm

Cut out

⅜in / 1.9cm

2in / 5cm

DOOR
Cut
out

Cut out

2⅛in / 5.3cm

4¼in / 10.7cm

cut out door from front only

7⅛in / 18cm

2⅛in / 5.3cm

DOOR Bake 2

1in / 2.5cm

BACK
Bake 1

5½in / 13.7cm

4¼in / 10.7cm

7⅛in / 18cm

1st STEP
Bake 1

2⅜in / 6cm

2in / 5cm

STEEPLE SIDES
Bake 2

2⅜in / 6cm

2⅛in / 5.3cm

TOP STEEPLE
COVER
Bake 1

2½in / 6.4cm

2½in / 6.4cm

2nd STEP
Bake 1

2in / 5cm

1¾in / 4.3cm

3rd STEP
Bake 1

2in / 5cm

1in / 2.5cm

STEEPLE front
& Back
Bake 2

1¾in / 4.2cm

2¼in / 5.8cm

2½in / 6.3cm

Simple Constructions

'Buy any gingerbread, gilt gingerbread.'
BEN JONSON Bartholomew Fayre

One of the great delights of designing with gingerbread is its versatility *and creative flexibility. Many household objects, utensils, ornaments or toys can be charmingly replicated, meaning that if you are planning gingerbread gifts you can personalize them to match the recipient's tastes and interests. For a hobbyist, a gingerbread toolbox could be fashioned, with a cut-out hammer, saw and wrench inside; for a child, a gingerbread building with an open front could be fitted out inside as a doll's house, or you could make a Wild West fort, or a racing car. The simple constructions in this chapter – a cookie bowl, a bird house, a woven basket, a Jack-in-the-Box and a treasure chest – illustrate some easy-to-use moulding, plaiting, modelling, and shaping techniques which could be readily adapted for any ideas of your own.*

OPPOSITE: *Gingerbread is quite a flexible foodstuff, and can be manipulated in various ways to create a variety of effects. As well as two- and three-dimensional constructions of various kinds, it can be moulded around objects to retain the shape when baked. Containers of gingerbread – such as the woven-look basket shown – are particularly attractive ways of presenting fruits, candies and sweets. Once the contents have been consumed, the box, basket or bowl can be eaten as well!*

Cookie Bowl

This completely edible bowl is a unique way to serve guests a variety of biscuits at afternoon tea; not only is it an impressive table decoration but it will also make an interesting conversation piece. This is a very simple project which can be made weeks ahead and filled just prior to serving.

Although it is presented as a cookie bowl, it may be filled with an assortment of other confections such as sweets, truffles, tea cakes, etc. By changing the colours and decorations used on the bowl, it can be made suitable for any occasion.

REQUIREMENTS

gingerbread pieces made with
1 × quantity of recipe 2 (see page 15)
9 in/22.5 cm diameter round board
3¹/₂ cups/1¹/₂lb/675g royal icing:
2 cups/³/₄lb/350g ivory
1 cup/¹/₂lb/225g moss green
¹/₂ cup/¹/₄lb/100g red
biscuits, cookies, candies, etc. (to fill the bowl)

This sumptuous bowl is deceptively impressive, being extremely simple to construct. You can mould a gingerbread bowl around differently shaped china and glass vessels for a variety of results. This bowl is decorated quite plainly, with a simple Christmas-theme trim around the lip and base of the board. You could, however, pipe decorations over the sides of the bowl as well, in colours to match the cookies or sweets to be displayed.

1 Cut out a card template to the dimensions required, and make the gingerbread piece. You will need just 1 circle, to match the size of your cake board. (The bowl itself does not require a template but you will need a china or glass bowl to mould the gingerbread around.) See page 67 for the outline, and page 20 for how to trace and make card templates.

2 Take a medium-sized ovenproof glass or china bowl, turn it upside down and cover it with sheets of foil, tucking the excess underneath the bowl. Cover the foil with a light coating of non-stick cooking spray. Place the bowl on top of a sheet of baking paper, placed on a baking or cookie sheet.

3 Roll out a large piece of gingerbread, big enough to cover the top and sides of the bowl. Gently drape the sheet of dough over the foil-covered bowl or basin.

4 With your hands, working from the top of the bowl down, gently work all the pleats out of the gingerbread to get a smooth single layer of dough over the entire bowl. Using a sharp knife, trim the excess dough from the bottom edge of the bowl. Bake in an oven preheated to 350°F/180°C/ gas 4 for 20–25 minutes, until golden brown. Remove from the oven and allow to cool completely. Turn the bowl over and lift it out of the baked gingerbread shell. If bits of the foil try to stay in the shell they can be carefully removed with your fingers.

5 You will need to stick the round gingerbread base to the cake board for more support. Pipe a circle of royal icing inside the perimeter of the cake board and gently attach the round of gingerbread to the board.

6 Now pipe a small swirl of royal icing in the centre of the round piece of gingerbread. Place the bottom of the gingerbread bowl down on the swirl of icing, making sure it sticks well.

7 With royal icing, decorate your cookie bowl. This bowl is trimmed with ivory zig-zags around the rim of the bowl and edge of the board, with clusters and garlands of holly accented with little red bows. (All techniques needed are shown on page 23.)

8 The edible cookie bowl can be made weeks ahead and can be refilled time and time again. It may be filled with an assortment of biscuits, truffles, sweets or even pastries.

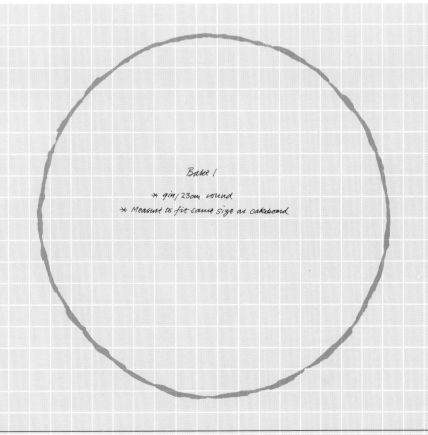

Bake 1

* 9in/23cm round
* Measure to fit same size as cakeboard

Bird House

This bird house was designed by constructing a scaled-down version of a basic house without all the doors and window openings. The front side has a round hole to allow the birds to come and go. This particular bird house is decorated with a spring theme, with bluebirds in front. It could also be done as a winter scene, perhaps adding robins or red cardinals instead of bluebirds.

By omitting the hole in the front wall and cutting out a door and window instead you could in fact construct a simple small house.

REQUIREMENTS

gingerbread pieces made with
$1/2$ × quantity of recipe 2 (page 15)
10 in/25 cm square board
$5^3/4$ cups/2lb 8oz/1.125kg royal icing:
2 cups/$^3/4$lb/350g yellow
1 cup/$^1/2$lb/225g brown
$1^1/2$ cups/10oz/300g moss green
$^1/2$ cup/$^1/4$lb/100g pink
$^1/4$ cup/2oz/50g white
$^1/2$ cup/$^1/4$lb/100g blue
yellow and white jelly beans (for the roof)

The completed bird house is simple to construct and decorative, but unusual and effective. It would be appropriate for a child's birthday or a special spring centrepiece, perhaps at Easter – it might be fun to include some surprise foil- or sugar-coated Easter eggs inside the bird house for children to discover.

1 Cut out card templates to the dimensions required and make the gingerbread pieces. You will need 2 pointed front and back pieces, one plain and one with a small cut-out circle; 2 identical wide rectangular side pieces; 2 rectangles for the roof; and 3 cut-out birds (see page 71 for the outlines, and page 20 for how to trace and make card templates).

2 Pipe a thin line of brown royal icing along the bottom edge of the back wall and place it down on the cake board, balancing it against a jar so both hands will be free. Pipe a thin line of icing along the sides and bottom edges of both the side pieces. Place 1 side piece against the back already standing. Repeat this procedure for the opposite wall. Pipe a thin line of icing along the bottom edge of the front of the house and place it down on the board, butting it up against the iced edges of the 2 sides already standing.

3 Pipe a line of brown icing along all the top edges of the 4 standing walls. Gently place 1 roof side and pipe a thin line of icing across the top edge of this. Place the second roof piece on, securing it to the 4 iced edges.

4 Once the bird house has been constructed, spread a thin layer of yellow royal icing on top of the roof to cover it completely. Using a continuous movement with a spatula, make long running streaks parallel with the long edges of the roof.

6 Using white royal icing, pipe a few scrolls and hearts on the front and back walls of the house for a little added decoration. Keep it simple-looking. With a spatula, ice the open cake board area with moss green royal icing. Immediately, before the icing begins to set, tap the icing with a flat spatula, lifting it up with a clean sharp motion to roughen the surface.

5 Place small coloured jelly beans along the top seam of the roof, pressing them into the fresh icing. Pipe a decorative zig-zag around the wall seams using brown royal icing. Then, with yellow icing, pipe a circle of stars around the front entrance hole and a zig-zag line along all the roof top edges.

7 With pink royal icing, pipe flowers on the roof corner and scatter a few throughout the yard. The birds are decorated with piped blue feathers and yellow beaks by using fill-in star piping (see page 23). Use fresh green icing to stick the decorated birds next to their bird house.

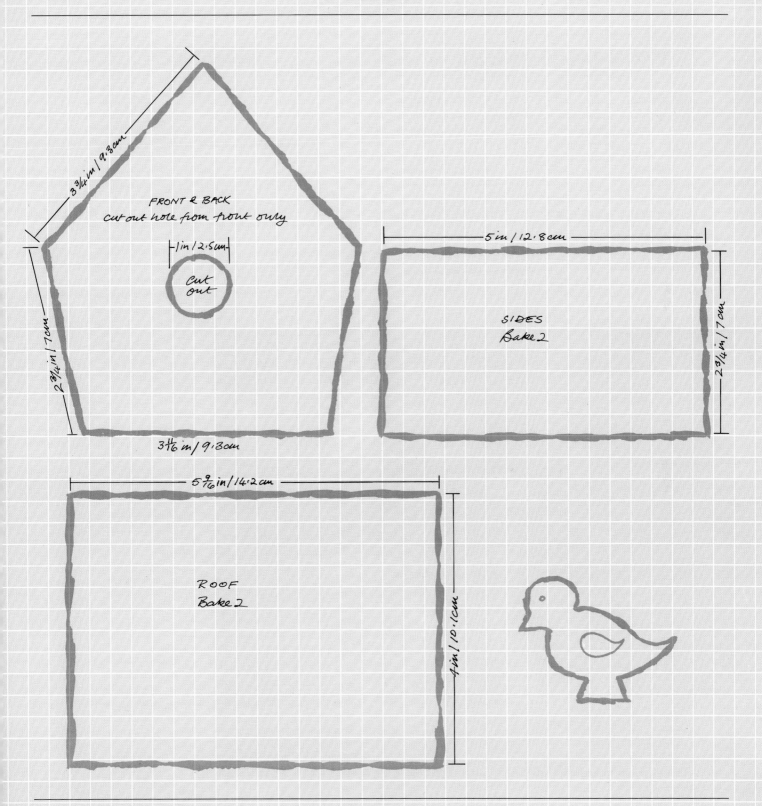

FRONT & BACK
cut out hole from front only

3 3/4 in / 9.3cm

1 in / 2.5cm

Cut out

2 3/4 in / 7cm

3 11/16 in / 9.30cm

5 in / 12.8cm

SIDES
Bake 2

2 3/4 in / 7cm

5 9/16 in / 14.2 cm

ROOF
Bake 2

4 in / 10.1cm

Woven Basket

This hexagonal woven basket proves how versatile gingerbread really can be. The sides were actually 'hand-woven', then baked to a golden brown. It would be a wonderful centrepiece for a bridal shower or afternoon tea, and a suitable everyday decoration for the dining room table.

Fill the basket with any number of items, depending on the theme of your celebration. Fresh fruits, dried flowers and truffles are a few possibilities. If a particular colour theme is wanted, ice an appropriately coloured bow carefully to the handle. Alternatively, simply select items to fill your basket that are of the shades required.

REQUIREMENTS

gingerbread pieces made with approx.
2 × quantity of recipe 2 (see page 15)
10 in/25 cm square board
3 cups/1¼lb/550g brown royal icing
dried flowers, fresh fruit, etc. (to fill the basket)

This woven basket is one of the most versatile of all the centrepieces shown in this book. Over the last few years, woven baskets have become very popular as wall-hangings and centrepieces to hold flowers, plants and any number of items. This gingerbread version is appropriate for every occasion. It is shown on page 63 filled with fresh fruit as an everyday decoration, and here filled with dried flowers for a Christmas arrangement. Evergreens, ivory flowers, berry branches etc. can all be used and a Christmas bow can be added to the handle for a final festive touch.

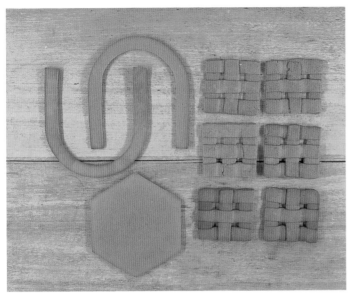

1 Cut out card templates to the dimensions required, and make the gingerbread pieces. You will need 1 hexagonal piece, and 2 arched frames for the handle (see page 75 for the outlines, and page 20 for how to trace and make card templates); you will also need 6 panels of woven gingerbread, each made from 6 thin strips as described in step 2.

2 Roll the gingerbread dough out to a thickness of ¼ in/ 6 mm on a sheet of parchment paper. Once the dough has been rolled out, use a pizza cutter to cut out 6 strips of gingerbread for each side of the basket (i.e. 36 in all), each about 4 × 1 in/10 × 2.5 cm.

3 On another sheet of parchment paper, draw six 4 in/10 cm squares. To make each basket side, first place 2 gingerbread strips vertically along the sides of a square. Then place 2 more strips horizontally on the top and bottom of the square. The gingerbread dough will overlap in the corners.

4 Next, place another strip vertically down the centre of the square of gingerbread, with the top and bottom overlapping. The last strip is now added by placing it horizontally in the centre of the box of gingerbread. You should now have 3 strips of gingerbread running vertically in the square and 3 strips running horizontally, all overlapping somewhat. Bake all 6 squares in an oven preheated to 350°F/ 180°C/gas 4 for 18–23 minutes, until golden brown. Nice crisp sharp edges will be needed to assemble the basket so the pieces may need to be trimmed slightly after baking.

5 The hexagonal base slab will now need to be attached to the cake board. Place a swirl of royal icing on the cake board and gently press the hexagonal bottom on the swirl of icing. This will prevent the basket from sliding.

7 To construct the handle, pipe dabs of icing along the inside centre of one of the handle pieces. Place the other handle piece directly on top and press them firmly together.

Using the brown royal icing, pipe a heavy line around the base of each handle piece. Then place the handle inside 2 opposite basket corners.

6 With the base secured to the cake board you can now begin to attach the basket sides to form the woven basket. Using brown royal icing, pipe a thin line along the bottom and right edge of each woven section and attach the bottom of each to the board, with the side edges meeting each other. Continue with all the sections until your basket is complete.

8 Using more brown royal icing, pipe a shell border around all the edges of the basket including the upper edge of the handle. Keeping the trim brown is in harmony with the woven effect, whereas using a bright vivid colour would actually distract from this. Allow the basket to dry for at least 24 hours before filling it.

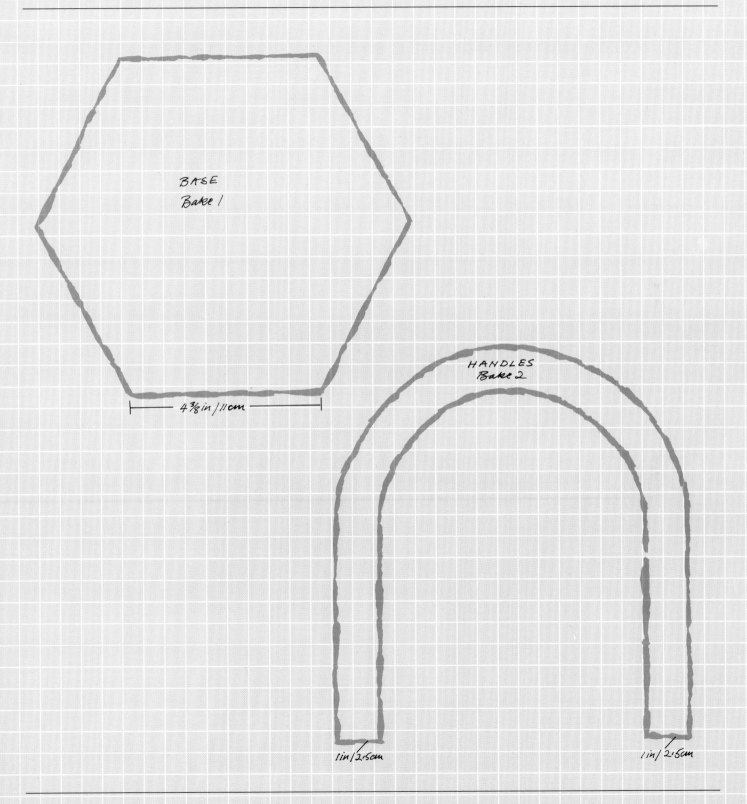

BASE
Bake 1

4⅜ in / 11 cm

HANDLES
Bake 2

1 in / 2.5 cm

1 in / 2.5 cm

Jack-in-the-Box

This is a delightful centrepiece for a child's birthday party. Two colour schemes are featured, the pastel shades being suitable for a younger child and the brighter and more vivid colours better for an older child. The letters piped on the sides of the box can be changed to numbers, possibly the age of the child.

REQUIREMENTS

gingerbread pieces made with
3 × quantity of recipe 1 (page 15)
10 in/25 cm square board, covered with foil paper
3¾ cups/1lb 10oz/725g royal icing:
¼ cup/2oz/50g red
2 cups/¾lb/350g ivory
¾ cup/6oz/175g burgundy
¼ cup/2oz/50g moss green
¼ cup/2oz/50g brown
¼ cup/2oz/50g orange
3 tbsp piping gel
60 silver or gold dragees
5 cups/4½lb/2kg granulated sugar or rice
3 sheets of tissue paper

This Jack-in-the-Box is an unusual and innovative gingerbread design, that is surprisingly straightforward to construct. It would make an appealing gift for a child's birthday – surprise sweets and candies could also be included in the box among the tissue paper. The box is decorated with a simple folk design, and the clown in vivid colours. Choose a colour scheme to suit the occasion.

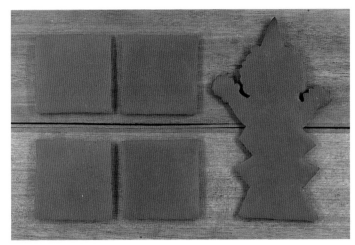

1 Cut out card templates to the dimensions required, and make the gingerbread pieces. You will need 4 squares for the sides and 1 cut-out clown figure (see page 79 for the outlines, and page 20 for how to trace and make card templates).

3 When all the lines have been covered with piping gel, turn the paper back over (piping gel side down) and line up the outer edges of the pattern with the gingerbread piece. Once lined up, gently lay the paper gel-side down directly on the gingerbread piece, and very lightly tap the paper down with your finger to ensure that the gel is attached to the gingerbread. When all the gel has stuck to the gingerbread, lift the paper straight up, leaving the gel lines on the gingerbread.

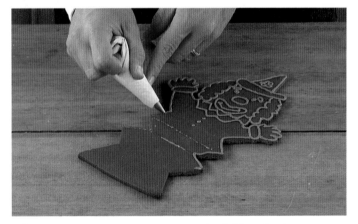

2 It is best to decorate the clown 24 hours before assembly, for easier handling. With your gingerbread clown baked and in front of you, you'll need to transfer the inner detail lines to it. Using a non-toxic marker, trace the clown pattern provided in the book on a blank sheet of paper to the size required. Turn the paper over and on the other side cover (or trace) all the lines with clear piping gel using a thin writing nozzle/tube.

4 Using coloured royal icing of your choice, pipe a line of icing over all the gel lines. This will provide an outline for all the features ready to be filled in with icing colours of your choice (see page 23 for the star fill-in method). Here the clown is decorated with ivory face and hands, a burgundy jacket with moss green trimmings, orange hair, and red trousers, hat and buttons.

5 With the 4 sides of the box and the cake board in front of you assemble the box by piping icing along the sides and bottoms and attaching the pieces together to form a square box. The box may then be decorated in a number of ways. Here, a red heart is first piped in the centre of all 4 sides, then a burgundy scalloped line is piped ⅝ in/1.5 cm in from the edge. Once that line is piped, pipe a row of ivory stars and, before they begin to set, press a gold dragee into the centre of each. A line of ivory stars is then piped all around the bottom trim, and an ivory zig-zag border piped along the side seams and top edge.

6 Leave the box to set for about 12 hours before filling. Place the dried gingerbread clown sitting up in the box, as if he were popping out. Pour granulated sugar or rice into the box to come two-thirds of the way up. This will be the support the clown needs to stand up.

7 Using tissue paper, make little puffs by cutting squares of tissue and holding them in the centre. Pull the corners up in a cluster and twist the tissue centre tightly between two fingers to form a point. This will make your ribbon-puffs hold together and fan out. Then randomly scatter the puffs throughout the open area in the box, pushing the twisted points down into the sugar.

A different colour scheme and pattern creates a completely new effect. In this variation, appropriate for a new baby or toddler's birthday, a pastel pink board covering was chosen, and pastel shades of pink, blue, yellow and lavender for the icing. Alphabet letters and flowers are piped on the box sides, giving the box the appearance of a learning cube.

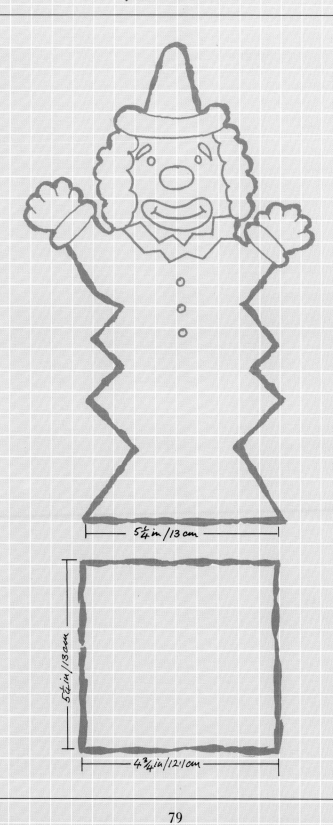

5¼ in / 13 cm

5¼ in / 13 cm

4¾ in / 12.1 cm

Treasure Chest

Wherever would-be pirates are, this treasure chest is sure to be a huge success. Stuffed to overflowing with candy jewels and chocolate coins, it makes an appropriate centrepiece for any child's birthday party. When selecting sweets with which to fill the chest, choose rich-looking ones, such as milk- and dark-chocolate truffles, available in a variety of shapes, and candies wrapped in gold and silver foil.

REQUIREMENTS

gingerbread pieces made with
1 × quantity of recipe 2 (page 15)
10 in/25 cm square board, covered with foil paper
3¼ cups/1lb 6oz/600g royal icing:
2½ cups/1lb/450g golden yellow
½ cup/¼lb/100g white
¼ cup/2oz/50g brown
2 striped candy sticks or canes (to support the lid)
48 gold or silver dragees
2 cups/8oz/225g brown sugar (for the sand)
truffles, chocolates, sweets, biscuits, etc. (to fill the chest)

An exotic treasure chest in a desert island setting – this is a simple construction, being a basic box shape, but is very effective. The chest can be filled with any number of sweets and candies, but this selection of rich truffles and gold and silver dragees is sumptuous and irresistible. Foil-wrapped gold chocolate coins would also look wonderful spilling out all over the sand.

1 Cut out card templates to the dimensions required, and make the gingerbread pieces. You will need 2 long rectangles for the sides; 2 slightly wider rectangles for the lid; 2 short rectangles for the chest ends; and 2 triangles for the lid ends (see page 83 for the outlines, and page 20 for how to trace and make card templates).

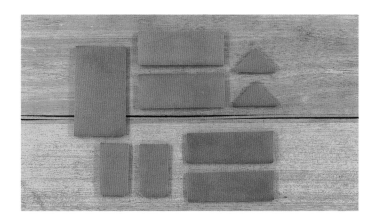

2 Assemble the lid and bottom of the treasure chest 24 hours before decorating it. To construct the lid, lay one of the long rectangle pieces flat. Pipe a line of royal icing along the top 2 edges of the two triangles and attach to both ends of the rectangle. Then pipe icing along one long side of the second long rectangular piece and place it against the other long piece, fitting it snugly to make a long 'roof' shape.

Attach the bottom of the treasure chest to the cake board with royal icing. Once that is secured, take one of the long rectangular sides, pipe a line of royal icing along the bottom edge and place it on the cake board directly next to the edge of the bottom piece. Next, pipe a line of icing along the bottom and sides of each of the 2 side pieces, and attach them neatly on top of the inside edge of the box.

3 Next, attach the remaining long rectangular piece to the front of the box – pipe a line of icing along the bottom edge and place it against the bottom edge of the platform, meeting the 2 sides but actually resting on the cake board.

Once these have dried thoroughly, you'll need something with which to prop open the lid of the treasure chest; candy sticks are ideal for this. Using a knife with a serrated edge, trim these with a sawing action to the required size. The longer they are, the more open your lid will be. Place a dab of royal icing on the bottom of each candy stick and attach to the bottom platform along the sides at an angle. You may prop them up with a couple of truffles or candies if need be while they are drying.

4 Next, pipe a large dab of icing on the top of each candy stick and a line of royal icing along the back top edge of the box. Carefully put the lid in position, resting the back edge along the line of icing and the front on the tops of the candy sticks or canes.

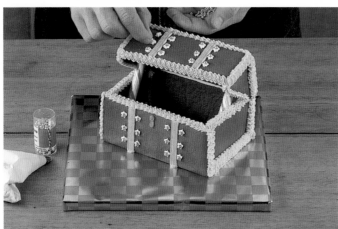

5 With the chest assembled and dried, you may decorate as you wish. Here the royal icing is coloured golden yellow and 2 strips have been piped on the front and back sides, and on the lid. Once these have been piped on, trim all the edges with a piped zig-zag border, and pipe on a brown lock. A line of white stars could be added on both sides of the piped strips, for more ornate decoration. Add gold dragees to the centres of the stars before they start to dry.

6 Scatter brown sugar thickly around the open space on the cake board to give a sandy beach effect. Then fill the chest with assorted rich dark truffles and foil-covered chocolate coins and candies.

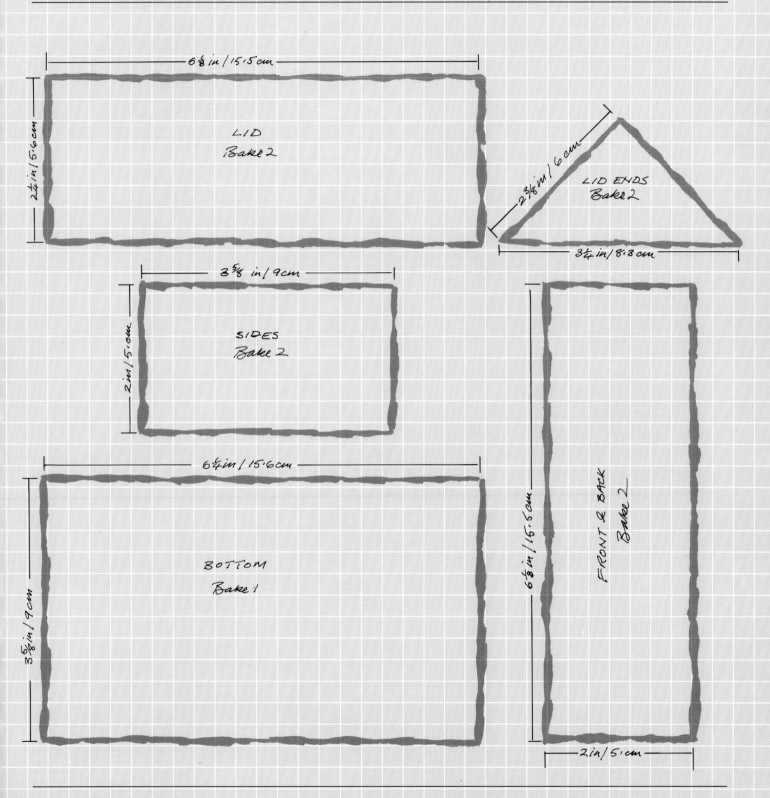

LID
Bake 2

6⅛ in / 15.5 cm

2¼ in / 5.6 cm

LID ENDS
Bake 2

2⅜ in / 6 cm

3¼ in / 8.3 cm

SIDES
Bake 2

3⅝ in / 9 cm

2 in / 5 cm

BOTTOM
Bake 1

6¼ in / 15.6 cm

3⅝ in / 9 cm

FRONT & BACK
Bake 2

6½ in / 16.5 cm

2 in / 5.1 cm

Grand Structures

'For him the gilt was yet on the gingerbread, the paint on the toy, the dew on the flower.'
WHYTE-MELVILLE Uncle John

Once you have mastered the basic techniques of gingerbread house *construction you will, like any good architect, want to attempt more ambitious projects. One simple variation on the house theme is the church on page 56, and virtually any other type of building or external structure can be made so long as you have the patience to develop the design and providing you can work out a successful method of construction. (I tried and failed many times, for example, before I found a way to stop my gazebo from falling over!) I have recreated many famous buildings in gingerbread, and, while making the Empire State Building, the Tower of London, the Eiffel Tower or the Taj Mahal may not be to your taste, the ability to scale down particular structures into manageable gingerbread creations is worth developing. The projects in this chapter evolved from subjects that captivated me: by following the more advanced techniques they illustrate, you will be able to go on to interpret ideas that have especially inspired you.*

OPPOSITE: *Gingerbread can be used to create airy, light constructions as well as solid-looking buildings. This delicate garden gazebo decorated with fancy lace ironwork cannot fail to impress. As with the grand Victorian mansion and fairground carousel, construction requires not so much skill and special technique as patience and time.*

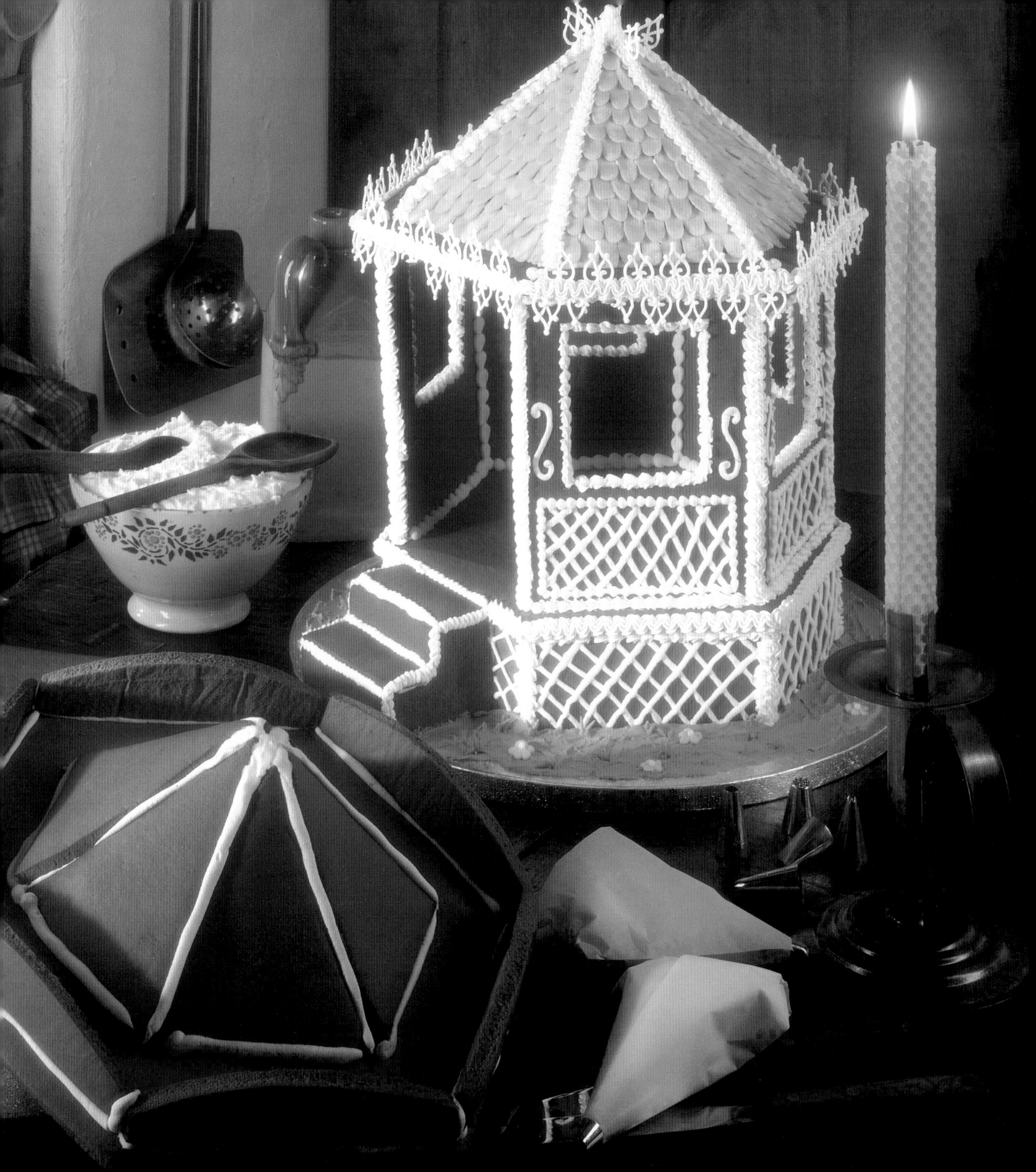

Carousel

A few years ago, I constructed this project for a competition in America and was so pleased with the outcome I wanted to repeat it for this book. The carousel made for the competition had a Christmas theme and was decorated with shades of red, green and white. Piped poinsettias, bells and scrolls were also added, and cut-out reindeer were substituted for the horses to enhance the festive theme.

This charming old-world carousel will bring back childhood memories. Decorated in traditional shades of ivory, mauve and burgundy, it is suitable for any birthday or special celebration.

REQUIREMENTS
gingerbread pieces made with at least
4 × quantity of recipe 2 (page 15)
16 in/40 cm diameter round board
5½ cups/2½lb/1.1kg royal icing:
3½ cups/1½lb/675g ivory
½ cup/¼lb/100g burgundy
1 cup/½lb/225g pink
½ cup/¼lb/100g moss green
1 ice-cream cone (to support the carousel)
6 striped candy sticks or canes
36 lace points (see page 26)

This gingerbread carousel is an incredible-looking construction – no-one will believe that it is completely edible! The decoration is in traditional Victorian fairground style, with red hearts, pink and green flowers, white scrolls, and white ornamental filigree 'ironwork'. For variety, a number of different animal-shaped cut-outs could be used.

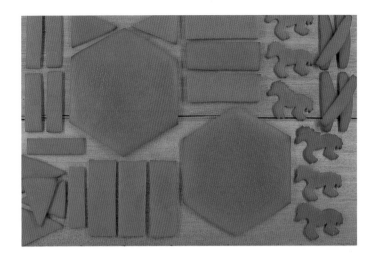

1 Cut out card templates to the dimensions required, and make the gingerbread pieces. You will need 2 large hexagonals for the base and top; 6 long rectangles for the central piece; 6 small rectangles for the bottom supports; 6 curved lengths for the top; 6 triangles for the roof; and at least 6 cut-out horses (allow extra for breakages). See page 91 for the outlines, and page 20 for how to trace and make card templates.

2 Steps 1–6 need to be completed 24 hours before the main construction and decoration to allow time for the structure to dry thoroughly.

Assemble the base support by first laying out the 6 short rectangular pieces on the cake board. As you construct the support, pipe a line of royal icing on the bottom and sides of the pieces and secure them to the board and each other. Royal icing dries quickly so you will need to pipe it on each piece just before you put it in place.

3 Once your hexagonal support is assembled on the cake board, pipe a thin line of icing completely around the top edge. Immediately centre your hexagonal slab on top and gently press it down on the supports. The piece will have a slight overhang to help give a 3-dimensional look.

4 With the 6 longer rectangle pieces at hand for the centre, pipe a thin line of icing on both long sides of each piece and place them together vertically. It is best to assemble this middle support on a covered cake board to avoid it sticking to the surface before transferring it to the main construction.

6 Pipe a line of royal icing on the bottom and sides of 1 curved piece. Secure the bottom of that piece to a side of the cover hexagon, resting it on top of the edge. Continue to pipe icing on each piece as you position them, until all 6 are fitted in place.

At this point it is wise to attach the horse cut-outs to the candy canes to give them time to dry. To do so, pipe a medium-sized dot of royal icing on the back of each horse. Position the horse in the middle of the shaft of the cane, so that the top hook is facing away from the horse.

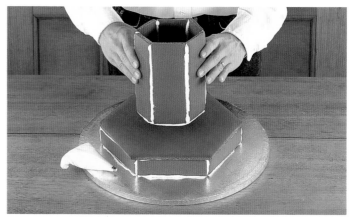

5 Construct the carousel cover by placing the other hexagonal slab of gingerbread directly in front of you. In the middle, place a 2 in/5 cm tall ice-cream cone for support (the cone is cut down using a sharp knife). Pipe a thin line of icing on the sides and bottom of one of the 6 triangular pieces. Gently press the shorter of the 3 sides down on to the hexagonal piece, keeping it lined up with the edge. The top point will then rest on the cone for support. Continue around until all 6 triangles are attached.

7 With the 3 pieces (base, middle and cover) dried thoroughly, the main construction can begin. Gently holding the middle in one hand, pipe a thin line of royal icing completely around its bottom edge. Looking directly down over it to ensure perfect positioning, centre it on the hexagonal base and press it down firmly to secure.

8 It is much easier to decorate the middle at this stage rather than wait and try to work around the poles and horses once they are in place. I have chosen burgundy hearts and ivory scrolls as side decorations, with an ivory zig-zag border for the side seams and a line of basic shells for the base border.

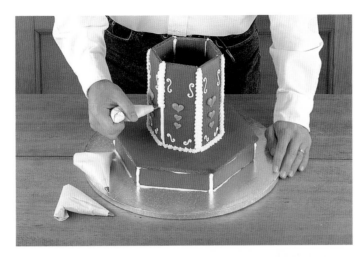

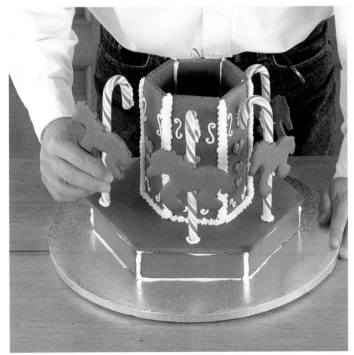

9 Attach the prepared horses and candy canes by piping a blob of icing on the bottom of each cane and on the outer edge of each hook. Position a candy cane in the centre of each section of the hexagon and press firmly in place.

10 Once the candy canes are in position you can move on to the decoration of each horse. Using burgundy royal icing, pipe the basic outline of each horse with a thin line. Then pipe on saddles and long flowing ivory lines for the manes and tails. With the same nozzle/tube, pipe zig-zags to fill in the hooves of the horses.

11 Pipe a wide line of icing completely around the edge of the middle section. Gently lift the cover of the carousel and centre it on top. Press down gently to secure it.

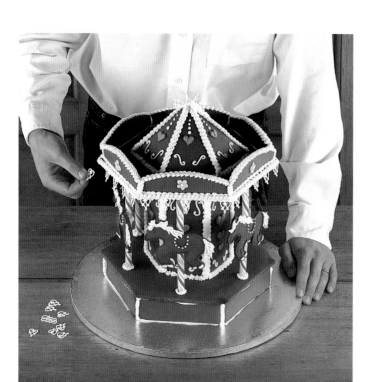

12 Decorate the cover of the carousel using the same theme chosen to decorate the middle section: burgundy hearts, ivory scrolls and dots, pink flowers and moss green leaves. Border all the curved edges with a piped ivory zig-zag, and pipe over all visible seams.

Carefully lift the prepared lace points from the board by sliding a thin knife gently underneath to release them. Attach these lace points to the freshly piped borders on the top of the cover and around the overhang before they begin to set.

13 Finish the carousel by decorating the base, keeping in mind the chosen theme to carry it through. Pipe a burgundy heart in the centre of each rectangular section and, using that as a central guide, pipe an ivory scroll on each side of the heart. Pipe each upper trim with an ivory zig-zag border and pipe a shell border around the bottom.

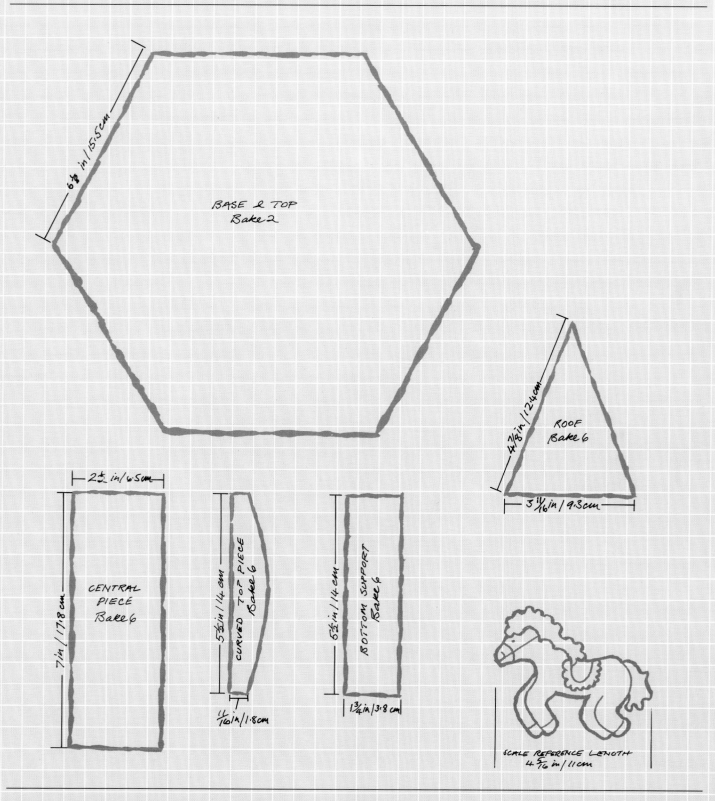

BASE & TOP
Bake 2

6⅛ in / 15.5 cm

ROOF
Bake 6

4⅞ in / 12.4 cm

3 ¹¹⁄₁₆ in / 9.3 cm

2½ in / 6.5 cm

CENTRAL
PIECE
Bake 6

7 in / 17.8 cm

CURVED TOP PIECE
Bake 6

5½ in / 14 cm

¹¹⁄₁₆ in / 1.8 cm

BOTTOM SUPPORT
Bake 6

5½ in / 14 cm

1¾ in / 3.8 cm

SCALE REFERENCE LENGTH
4 ⁵⁄₁₆ in / 11 cm

Gazebo

While visiting my grandparents in Iowa one Sunday, we were on our usual route to church and passed by the city park. My grandmother noticed the fancy white gazebo set directly in the centre of the park and asked me about making a gazebo from gingerbread.

My first thought was that this would be impossible because of the need for support, but the more I thought of it the more I became determined to try it. After several attempts at different structural designs and methods, the gazebo was eventually created.

To add a springtime look to a centrepiece, you could arrange a small posy of fresh, silk or dried flowers inside the gazebo.

REQUIREMENTS

gingerbread pieces made with
4 × quantity of recipe 2 (page 15)
16 in/40 cm diameter round board
1 ice-cream cone (to support the gazebo)
5½ cups/2¼lb/1kg royal icing:
3 cups/1¼lb/550g white
2 cups/¾lb/350g gooseberry or moss green
½ cup/¼lb/100g pink
1 cup/1lb/450g flaked almonds
95 lace points (see page 26)

This enchanting ornamental Victorian gazebo looks as if it has just been lifted out of a summer garden. The use of silvered almonds for tiles, and lace points for filigree ironwork, are particularly realistic. This creation makes an elegant centrepiece for a summer table or celebration, and could be filled with sprays of sugar flowers in complementary colours of ivory, pale green and pink.

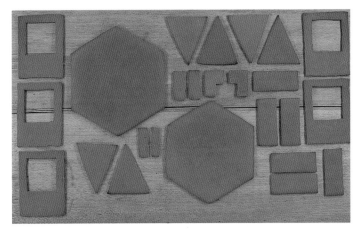

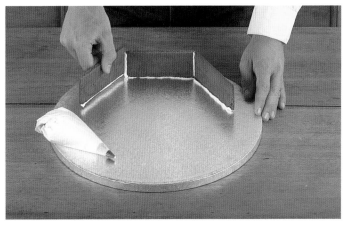

1 Cut out card templates to the dimensions required, and make the gingerbread pieces. You will need 2 large hexagonals of different sizes for the base and top; 5 wide rectangles for the side walls, each with a large window area; 6 triangles for the roof; 6 small rectangles for the base walls; and 4 rectangles and 2 L-shapes for the steps (see page 97 for the outlines, and page 20 on how to trace and make card templates).

2 Try to complete steps 1–6 of the gazebo at least 48 hours prior to adding the top and decoration. This allows ample time for it to dry thoroughly.

To construct the base, first position the 6 rectangular pieces on the cake board. Pipe a line of royal icing on the bottom and sides of 1 rectangular piece and attach it to the board, then do the same with the other 5. Royal icing dries quickly, so pipe each piece as you use it.

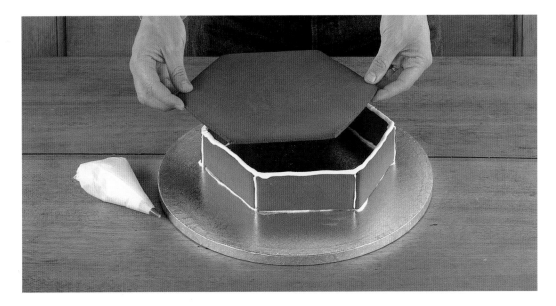

3 Once your hexagonal support is assembled on the cake board, pipe a thin line of icing completely around the top edge. Immediately centre the smallest of the 2 hexagonal slabs over the top of the support and gently press it down to secure it firmly.

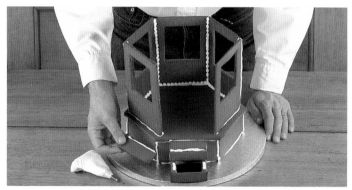

4 Place the larger of the 2 hexagonal slabs in front of you. From each of the corners measure 1 in/2.5 cm inwards towards the centre and mark each spot with a piped dot of royal icing. These will serve as guides when assembling the triangles to form the cover. Place a 3 in/7.5 cm ice-cream cone in the centre of the hexagon to serve as a support for the triangles (the cone is cut down using a sharp knife). Pipe each triangular piece and place it, bottom side down, between 2 of the guide dots, letting the top lean inward to rest on the cone.

6 At this point, while access to the interior is easier, pipe a line of shells with royal icing along all the inner seams of the gazebo. Assemble the steps to the gazebo by piping a line of icing along the back and bottom of both side supports. Place these against the gazebo base, centred in front of the entrance and 2¾ in/6.5 cm apart. Pipe a medium line of icing along all the edges of the 2 side step pieces left uncovered. Then, place in position the 2 rectangular pieces for the fronts of the steps, followed by the top 2 rectangular pieces for the tops of the steps.

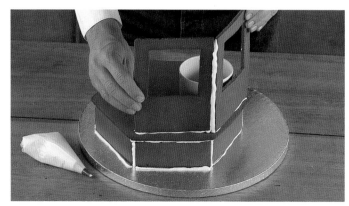

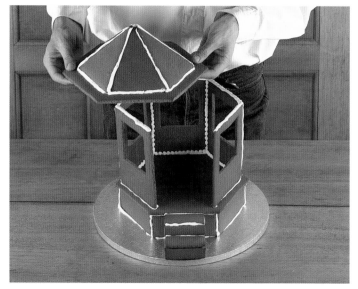

5 With the smaller hexagonal base previously constructed in front of you, now add the 5 walls of the gazebo. Pipe a line of icing along the bottom and left-hand side of each section of wall. Place 1 wall bottom-side down (the window area is the upper part of the wall) on the base, 1 in/2.5 cm in from the edge. Continue around the base with 3 more walls. For the 5th and final wall, pipe the icing on the bottom and right-hand side and connect it to the other 4 walls. In this way, you will have no icing showing on the front edges of the entrance.

7 Once the side walls are set and have had ample time to dry, pipe a medium line of icing completely along the top edges of each wall. Then, centre the hexagonal cover directly on top of the 5 walls.

8 To simulate shingles on the cover, pipe lines of royal icing and stick pieces of flaked almonds side-by-side along these lines. When piping the next row, make it only about half the length of an almond up from the last line to allow the almonds to overlap. It is best to start from the bottom of the triangle and work upwards to the point for a neat overlapping effect.

9 Once all the almonds have been placed on the cover of the gazebo, pipe a zig-zag border of white royal icing along each seam. Do not be concerned if you are covering up any almonds as you do want to hide the outer edges of the almond rows.

10 Next, begin to decorate the gazebo. Using white royal icing, pipe hearts on each of the corners of the hexagonal top, trim the window edges with a shell border and pipe decorative scrolls on the sides. Pipe lattice squares below the windows and then on each base support wall (see page 24 for techniques).

11 Once all of the lattice-work has been piped on, trim all of the edges and seams of the gazebo with a zig-zag border. Work from the bottom to the top, finishing off with the cover edge.

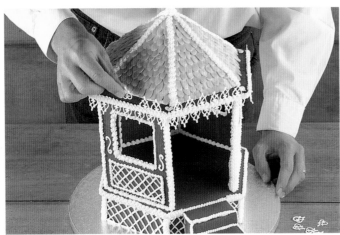

12 Immediately, while the cover edge trim is still fresh, add your prepared lace points to that trim. Lace points can be placed on both the top (pointing upwards) and the bottom (pointing down) of the border. Or, if you prefer, you may do one or the other. Place them also at the top point of the cover.

13 Add a layer of royal icing coloured gooseberry or moss green to the exposed top of the cake board, leaving 'thumb room' on the inner edge of the board. While your icing is still fresh, use a spatula to touch the icing gently, lifting and pulling directly up to create small peaks.

Little pink piped drop flowers can be scattered throughout the yard. You may also choose to add trees or shrubs.

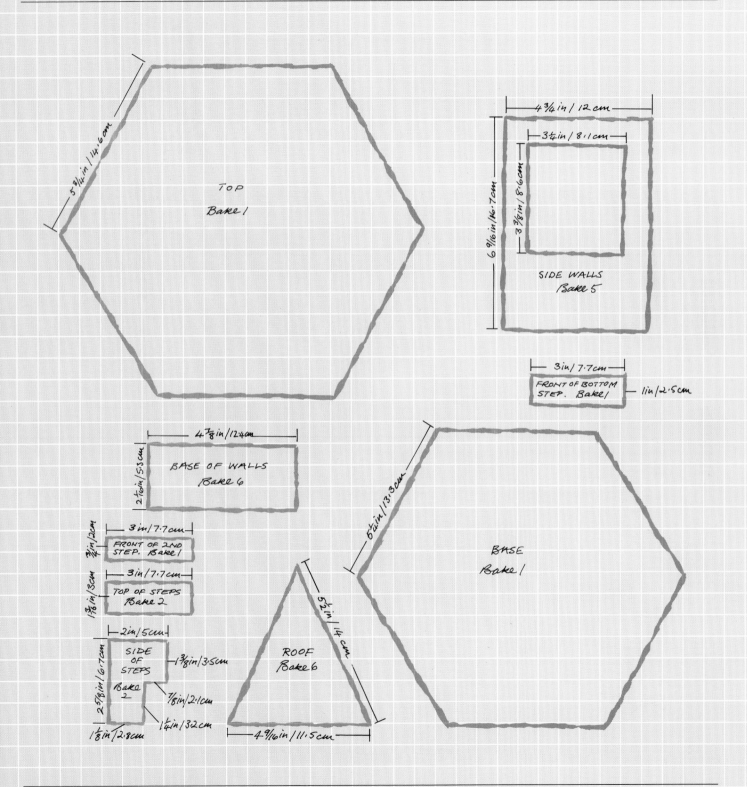

TOP
Bake 1

5 ¾ in / 14.6 cm

SIDE WALLS
Bake 5

4 ¾ in / 12 cm

3 ¼ in / 8.1 cm

3 ⅜ in / 8.6 cm

6 ⁹⁄₁₆ in / 16.7 cm

FRONT OF BOTTOM
STEP. Bake 1

3 in / 7.7 cm

1 in / 2.5 cm

BASE OF WALLS
Bake 6

4 ⅞ in / 12.4 cm

2 ⅛ in / 5.3 cm

FRONT OF 2ND
STEP. Bake 1

3 in / 7.7 cm

¾ in / 2 cm

TOP OF STEPS
Bake 2

3 in / 7.7 cm

⅞ in / 3 cm

SIDE
OF
STEPS

Bake
2

2 in / 5 cm

1 ⅜ in / 3.5 cm

⅞ in / 2.1 cm

2 ⅝ in / 6.7 cm

1 ¼ in / 3.2 cm

1 ⅛ in / 2.8 cm

ROOF
Bake 6

5 ½ in / 14 cm

4 ⁹⁄₁₆ in / 11.5 cm

BASE
Bake 1

6 ½ in / 13.3 cm

Victorian Mansion

lthough this Victorian country house is on the 'grand' scale, don't let that put you off attempting to construct one. It may look large and impressive, but the fact remains that it is only a basic house with small additions to give a more grandiose effect.

The decoration of this house is all based on simple techniques; all that is required is some time and a little effort! The overall scene was sprinkled lightly with powdered sugar to give the look of newly fallen snow.

The large Victorian mansion is probably the most complex construction project in the book, but the techniques of assembly are nonetheless the same as for a simple building. If taken in stages, step-by-step, it is quite achievable. The house is full of nooks and crannies to explore and discover, such as verandahs, porches, dormer windows, and ornamental ironwork. In gingerbread competitions, such mansions are often constructed twice this size or more.

REQUIREMENTS

gingerbread pieces made with
2 × quantity of recipe 2 (page 15)
24 × 18 in/60 × 46 cm board,
covered in red foil paper
10¹/₂ cups/4¹/₂lb/2.025kg royal icing:
6¹/₂ cups/2³/₄lb/1.25kg white
2¹/₂ cups/1lb/450g moss green
1 cup/¹/₂lb/225g brown
¹/₂ cup/¹/₄lb/100g red
sheet gelatine (for the windows)
4 striped candy sticks or canes (for the pillars)

12oz/350g chocolate-covered raisins
(for the chimney stones)
1lb/450g package of red and green jellies or gum drops
(for the roof)
48 lace points (see page 26)
¹/₄ cup/8oz/225g chocolate buttons (for the pathway)
2 ice-cream cones (for the trees)
4 marshmallows (for the bushes)
1 chocolate flake (for the logs)
¹/₂ cup/2¹/₂oz/75g caster or superfine sugar (for the snow)

1 Cut out card templates to the dimensions required, and make the gingerbread pieces. You will need 2 long rectangles for the front and back wall, one with 1 door and 2 windows; 2 pointed side walls (+ 1 optional extra to add strength); 2 long rectangles for the roof, with indentations; 2 side wall rectangles, one with a window, 1 pointed wall with 2 arched windows, and 2 trapezoid-shaped roof pieces, for the front extension; 2 small side walls, one with a window; 2 roof squares; and 1 small pointed wall with door and arched window, for the back porch; 3 doors; 2 long L-shapes for the front verandah; 2 chimney pieces; and 6 shutters (see page 103 for the outlines, and page 20 for how to trace and make card templates).

2 Place gelatine on the backs of all the windows of the house as shown on page 27, turn over and pipe a line of white dots around the trim of all the windows. Pipe a line of royal icing along the bottom and right edge of the plain back wall and attach it to the far back side of the board. Take one of the pointed side walls and butt it up against the back wall now standing. Take the front wall and position it on the board. Pipe a line of icing along both left edges of the front and back.

Butt the final pointed side wall against the 2 freshly piped side edges. If you like, insert an extra pointed side wall inside the construction to help support the walls and roof.

Pipe a line of icing along all the top edges. Place the back piece of the roof on, making sure that the smaller cut-out section is on the far back corner of the house. For the front piece, pipe and position it on so that the small cut-out part is to the far side and the larger cut-out piece to the front.

3 The front extension is now added by piping icing along the bottom and left edge of the extension side wall with the window, and lining it up with the cut-out portion of the roof. Repeat this for the opposite extension side wall with no window. Once these are up, pipe a line of icing along the front edges and place the front extension wall on. Run a line of icing along the longest edges of the trapezoid roof extension pieces and place both on. Pipe a line of icing along the top seam.

4 To construct the back porch, pipe a line of icing along the right and bottom edges of a porch side wall and place it in position so that it is off centre towards the back of the house side wall. Repeat for the other windowed porch wall. Pipe icing along the bottom edges of the front porch piece and the front edges of the standing side porch walls, and attach the front. Then pipe a line of icing around all the top edges and place the porch roof pieces in place.

5 Pipe a dot trim around both the sides and the top of the doors and adhere them to the door frame so that they are slightly ajar; 1 on the back porch and 2 either side of the main door. Pipe dots for door handles on each. Pipe green trailing holly with red berries around the doors (see page 23 for techniques).

Place the L-shaped verandah base in front of the house, fitting it in snugly and securing on to the board with icing. Cut the hooks off the candy canes (the height depends on how high you want the porch to be), and fix the cut candy sticks on to the main porch base with dabs of royal icing. Pipe holly cascading down around the pillars. To add the main porch top, place dabs of icing on the tops of the candy sticks and pipe a line of icing along the long back edge and longest side edge of the piece. Attach it against the house, resting on the candy pillars.

6 To fix on the chimney, pipe royal icing along the back of the chimney piece and adhere it to the side of the house. Repeat this for the other chimney piece and attach it directly on top of the first one, with both tops of the chimney fitting into the section cut in the roof.

8 Cut the jellies or gum drops in half ready to be placed on the roof. Spread a thin layer of white icing over the main roof, back porch and front extension. Place the sweets in rows, alternating the colours as you attach them to the back porch, front extension and main roof. Pipe a line of royal icing along the top point seams of these roofs as you go and gently attach the lace points, pointing upwards.

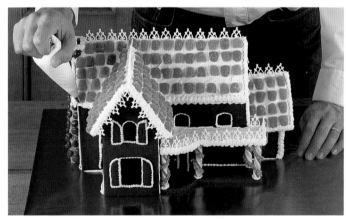

7 Spread a layer of brown royal icing over all parts of the chimney and, before the icing begins to set, attach chocolate-covered raisins to represent stones.

9 Pipe a white zig-zag border around the eaves of all the roof pieces and chimney edges. While the borders are fresh, attach lace points where preferred, pointing upwards and downwards. Add shutters by piping a dab of royal icing to the back of the pieces and then attaching them to the sides of the window. Trim with a series of dots. Spread white icing over the front verandah roof.

10 Pipe green holly and red bows around the tops of the windows, and red scrolls on the fronts of the shutters.

12 Using white royal icing, pipe icicles along the top edges and centre sections of the roof, as shown on page 24.

11 Spread a thin layer of white royal icing around the yard with a spatula, using a swirling motion. While the icing is still fresh, place chocolate buttons for the pathways and position the prepared trees and bushes (see page 26 for techniques). Position the cut chocolate flake logs by the back porch for a woodpile.

13 With a small strainer, sieve caster or superfine sugar over the entire finished house, tapping gently with your finger to let the sugar fall all around like snow.

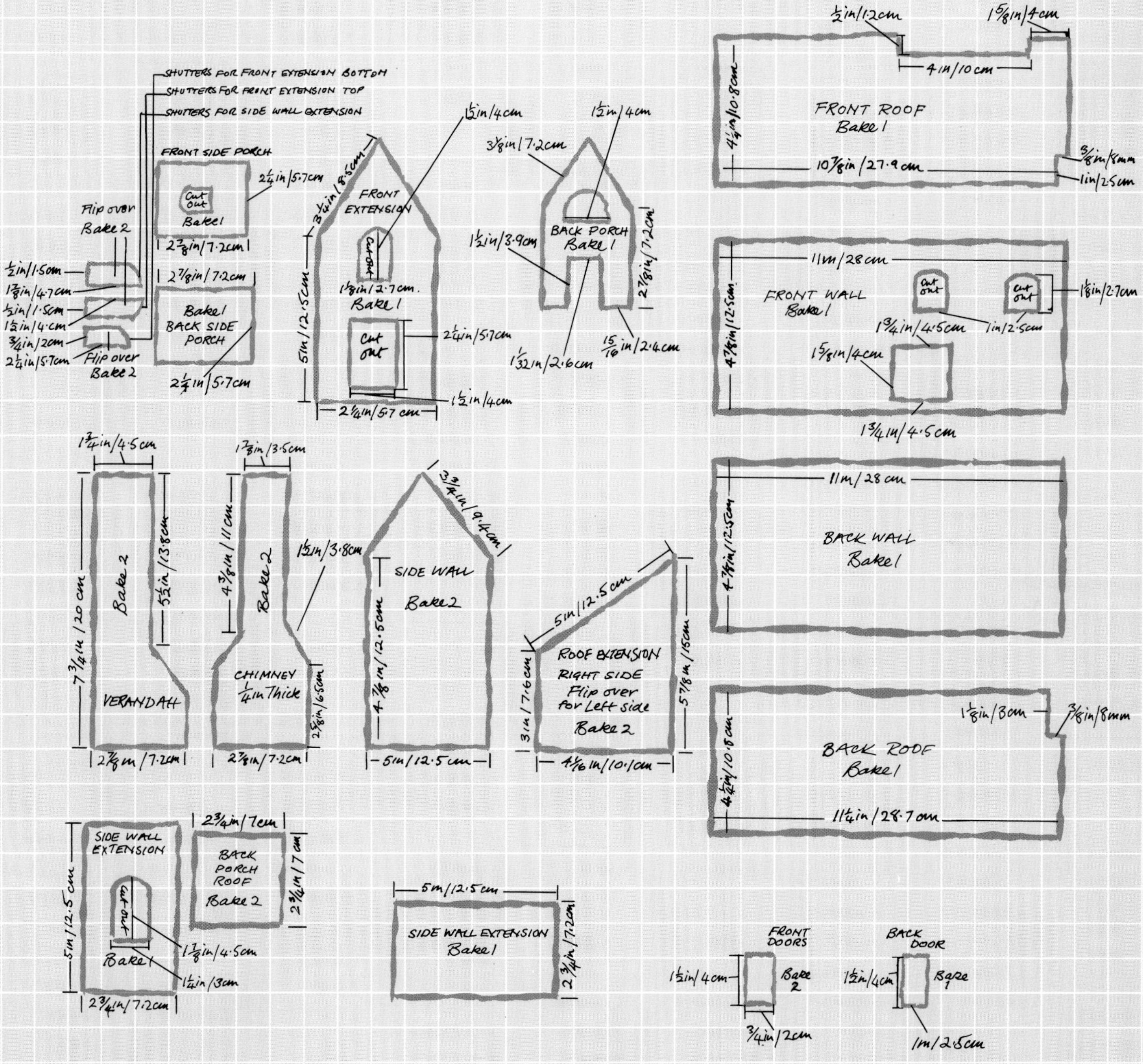
SHUTTERS FOR FRONT EXTENSION BOTTOM
SHUTTERS FOR FRONT EXTENSION TOP
SHUTTERS FOR SIDE WALL EXTENSION
FRONT SIDE PORCH
Cut out
Bake 1
2¼in/5.7cm
2⅞in/7.2cm
Flip over Bake 2
½in/1.5cm
1⅞in/4.7cm
½in/1.5cm
1½in/4cm
¾in/2cm
2¼in/5.7cm
Flip over Bake 2
2⅞in/7.2cm
Bake 1 BACK SIDE PORCH
2¼in/5.7cm
FRONT EXTENSION
3¼in/8.5cm
1½in/4cm
Cut out
1⅛in/2.7cm.
Bake 1
Cut out
2¼in/5.7cm
5in/12.5cm
1½in/4cm
2¼in/5.7cm
BACK PORCH Bake 1
1½in/4cm
3⅛in/7.2cm
1½in/3.9cm
2⅞in/7.2cm
15/16in/2.4cm
1 1/32in/2.6cm
½in/1.2cm
1⅝in/4cm
4in/10cm
FRONT ROOF Bake 1
4¼in/10.8cm
10⅞in/27.9cm
3/8in/8mm
1in/2.5cm
11in/28cm
FRONT WALL Bake 1
Cut out
Cut out
1⅛in/2.7cm
4⅞in/12.5cm
1in/2.5cm
1¾in/4.5cm
1⅝in/4cm
1¾in/4.5cm
1¾in/4.5cm
Bake 2
7¾in/20cm
5½in/13.8cm
VERANDAH
2⅞in/7.2cm
1⅜in/3.5cm
4⅜in/11cm
Bake 2
1½in/3.8cm
CHIMNEY ¼in Thick
2⅝in/6.5cm
2⅞in/7.2cm
3¾in/9.4cm
SIDE WALL Bake 2
4⅞in/12.5cm
5in/12.5cm
5in/12.5cm
ROOF EXTENSION RIGHT SIDE Flip over for Left side Bake 2
3in/7.6cm
5⅞in/15cm
4 1/16in/10.1cm
11in/28cm
BACK WALL Bake 1
4⅞in/12.5cm
BACK ROOF Bake 1
1⅛in/3cm
3/8in/8mm
4¼in/10.8cm
11¼in/28.7cm
SIDE WALL EXTENSION
Cut out
5in/12.5cm
1⅞in/4.5cm
1¼in/3cm
Bake 1
2¾in/7.2cm
2¾in/7cm
BACK PORCH ROOF Bake 2
2¾in/7cm
5in/12.5cm
SIDE WALL EXTENSION Bake 1
2¾in/7.2cm
FRONT DOORS
1½in/4cm
Bake 2
¾in/2cm
BACK DOOR
1½in/4cm
Bake 1
1in/2.5cm

Novelty Centrepieces

'I gave my love a bonnet blue,
A posy wove in red,
I gave to her 'My own true love',
Spelt on a gingerbread.'
OLD FOLK SONG

Gingerbread can be made throughout the year, and there are constructions in this book to suit every conceivable occasion. However, to add a finishing touch, I have created special novelty festival centrepieces for our principal traditional celebrations.
Most of the gingerbread projects illustrated earlier are very attractively adapted as Christmas or Easter centrepieces with the use of appropriate decorative work and suitable styling and propping, but it is also pleasing to have something slightly different, such as the Easter Basket and Christmas Sleigh given here.
The Hallowe'en creation is a basic house form, and you can have a great deal of fun in making it look as run down and dilapidated as you like. This is one of the most enjoyable projects to make, and children will love to help with the ghost and ghoul cut-outs.
The Valentine heart box is one of my particular favourites. It not only makes a very romantic gift on February 14, but is also ideal for many other occasions during the year – from weddings and anniversaries, to engagement parties and Mother's Day.

OPPOSITE: *Any traditional festival or important personal occasion will be made extra-special with a thematic gingerbread creation. Hallowe'en, Thanksgiving, Christmas, Easter, Mothering Sunday – all lend themselves to novel ideas that can be attractively presented in gingerbread form, as gifts or wonderful table centrepieces.*

Valentine Heart Box

REQUIREMENTS

gingerbread pieces made with
1 × quantity of recipe 1 (page 15)
12 in/30 cm heart-shaped board
6 cups/2¹/₂lb/1.125kg royal icing:
2¹/₂ cups/1lb/450g white
2 cups/³/₄lb/350g pink
1 cup/¹/₂lb/225g red
¹/₂ cup/¹/₄lb/100g green
38 lace points (see page 26)
15–20 moulded gingerbread biscuits or cookies
(to fill the box); see page 30

S t. Valentine's Day is a day to show those around you how much you really care. This gingerbread heart box makes a perfect gift. It may be filled with any number of goodies such as biscuits, chocolate truffles, etc., keeping in mind the favourite treats of the recipient.

As the heart is the symbol of love, this box may also be created as a centrepiece for a bridal shower or wedding. Decorate the box in the chosen theme colours of the occasion and pipe the names of the bride and groom on the lid to add a personal touch.

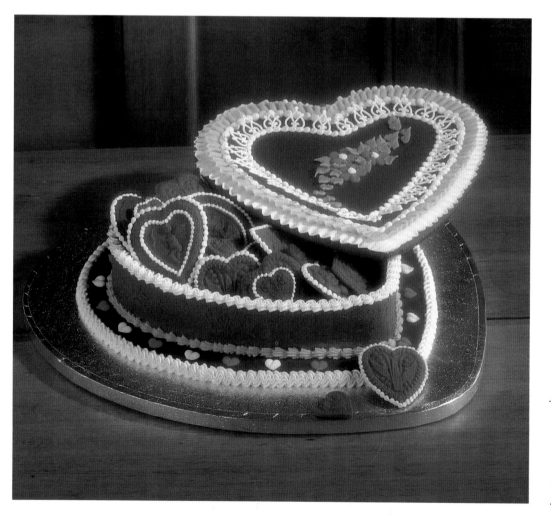

This sumptuous heart-shaped box is a visual delight and is also an unusual way of presenting and displaying biscuits or chocolates for a special gift. The lace, hearts and flowers decoration is traditional and romantic – as is the colour scheme of pink, red and white. The ornamentation and colours can be adapted for other occasions. Fill the box to overflowing with home-made gingerbread goodies.

1 Cut out card templates to the dimensions required, and make the gingerbread pieces. You will need 2 heart shapes, one larger than the other; and a heart-shaped ring, made by moulding gingerbread inside a tin as described in step 2 (see page 109 for the outlines, and page 20 for how to trace and make card templates).

2 To make the frame, lightly grease the sides of a 9 in/23 cm heart-shaped cake tin. Cut 2 strips, 2 in/5 cm wide and each about 18 in/46 cm long, and use these to line the inside edge of the tin. Press the seams together, and bake in an oven 350°F/180°C/gas 4 for 18–20 minutes. Allow to cool completely in the pan before gently lifting out.

3 Pipe a swirl of royal icing on the cake board then position the larger of the 2 heart pieces, pressing it on.

4 Take the frame of the heart box and pipe a line of royal icing along the entire bottom edge. Centre it on the gingerbread heart.

5 Pipe a white zig-zag border around the edge of the base and the top edge of the box. Pipe a pink shell border along the bottom edge of the box.

Alternating colours as you go, pipe white hearts and red hearts, about 1 in/2.5 cm apart from one another, on the upper part of the base.

6 Using white and pink royal icing, pipe 2 rows of ruffle border on the outer edge of the small heart (the lid). Next pipe a white zig-zag trim in the inner edge of the ruffle to cover its edge. Pipe a series of white dots 1 in/2.5 cm in from the ruffle. Before the icing sets, insert lace points at an angle of 45°.

Pipe 3 red drop flowers with white centres in the middle of

the lid, and pipe green leaves spraying out from the flowers. Then fill the box with moulded cookies and candies, simply edged with white icing. Rest the lid carefully on top.

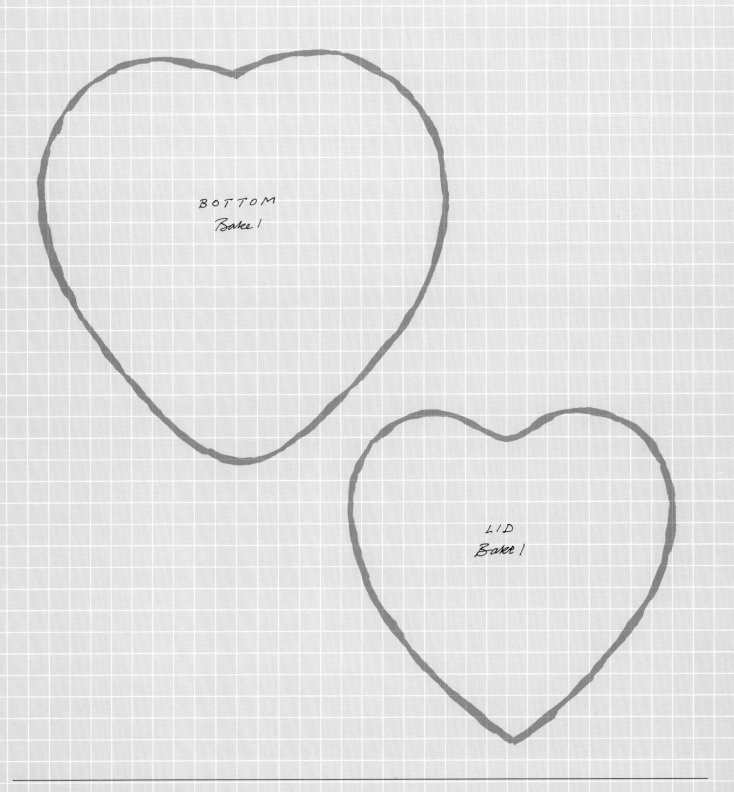

BOTTOM
Bake 1

LID
Bake 1

Easter Basket

The night before Easter, the Easter Bunny is said to visit all children while they are fast asleep to leave them something special. I can remember, as a child, filling a basket with grass the night before Easter and waking up to find it filled with chocolate chicks and bunnies, foil-covered eggs and all sorts of other treats.

This project is a very simple one to construct and decorate. With a little help, any child could complete this basket to set out ready for the Easter Bunny to fill.

REQUIREMENTS

gingerbread pieces made with
2 × quantity of recipe 2 (page 15)
10 in/25 cm diameter board
4 cups/1¾lb/750g royal icing:
3 cups/1¼lb/550g pink
¼ cup/2oz/50g pale yellow
¼ cup/2oz/50g pale lavender
½ cup/¼lb/100g light moss green
'Easter grass' or shredded tissue paper
eggs, candies, etc. (to fill the basket)
1 yard/1 metre yellow ribbon (for the bow)

A special Easter basket can be used as a centrepiece for an Easter celebration meal, or as a special gift. Decorate it with appropriate spring-like colours such as pale shades of pink, lemon and violet. Trim the handles with matching ribbon, and fill the basket with fresh or boiled eggs, perhaps ones you have hollowed and painted, or sugar eggs, chocolate chicks and bunnies.

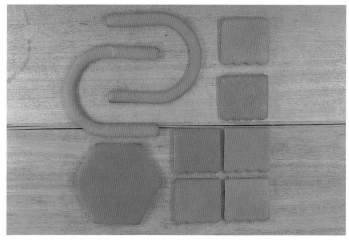

1 Cut out card templates to the dimensions required, and make the gingerbread pieces. You will need 1 hexagon; 6 squares with zig-zag edges for the sides; and 2 arched frames for the handles (see page 113 for the outlines, and page 20 for how to trace and make card templates).

2 Pipe a swirl of royal icing in the centre of the cake board. Place the hexagonal base of the basket on the icing, centred on the board, and press down gently. This will adhere to the board and prevent the basket from sliding once assembled.

3 Next pipe a line of royal icing along the bottom and right edge of one side section of the basket. Place the bottom down on the board against the edge of the hexagonal base. Continue this with the 5 remaining sides until the basket is complete and standing.

4 To construct the handle, pipe dabs of icing along the inside centre of 1 handle piece. Place the other handle piece directly on top and press them firmly together.

6 Trim all the edges and seams of the basket using pale pink royal icing. A star border is used along the bottom edge of the basket, and a zig-zag border is used to cover the other seams and edges.

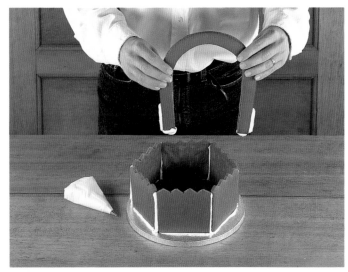

5 Pipe heavy lines of icing along the bottom and outside edge of the lower part of the handle. Then place the handle inside the basket so that it rests on the base and touches opposite corners.

7 Using the techniques shown on page 25, you can now decorate your Easter basket. Sprays of piped drop flowers in pastel colours – pale pink, yellow and lavender – and pale green leaves are added as decoration to the sides. Once assembled, the basket can be filled with Easter grass or shredded tissue paper, ready for goodies to be placed inside. Tie a decorative ribbon loosely around the handle.

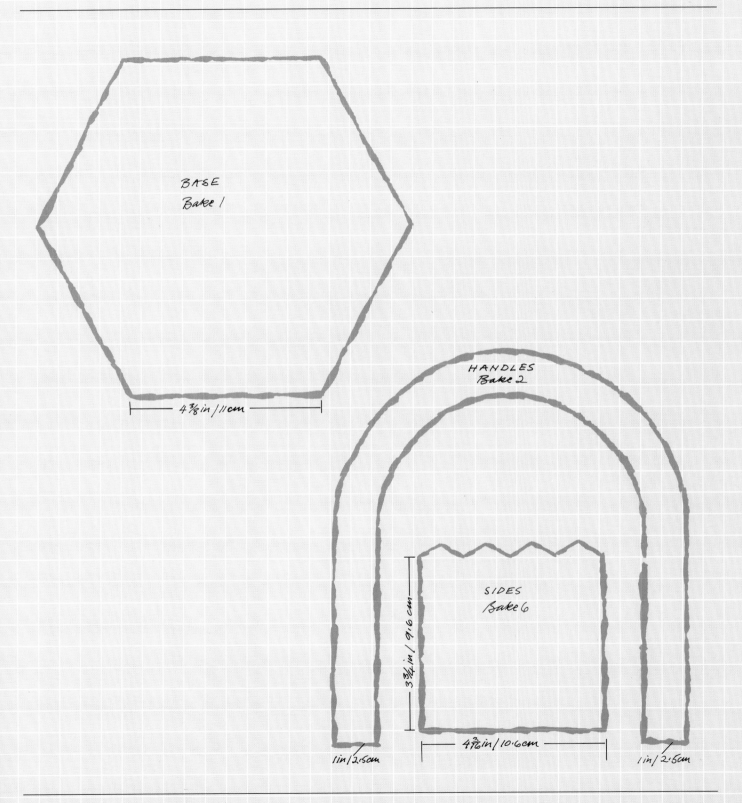

BASE
Bake 1

4⅜in / 11cm

HANDLES
Bake 2

SIDES
Bake 6

3¾in / 9.6 cm

4¾in / 10.6cm

1in / 2.5cm

1in / 2.5cm

Christmas Sleigh

REQUIREMENTS
gingerbread pieces made with
1 × quantity of recipe 2 (page 15)
12 × 15 in/30 × 37.5 cm board, covered with foil paper
7¹/₂ cups/3¹/₄lb/1.45kg royal icing:
3 cups/1¹/₄lb/550g white
2 cups/³/₄lb/350g ivory
1 cup/¹/₂lb/225g brown
1 cup/¹/₂lb/225g moss green
¹/₂ cup/¹/₄lb/100g red
chocolate and foil-wrapped truffles (to fill the sleigh)

The traditional sleigh has become an enduring symbol of Christmas. This sleigh makes an unusual centre-piece for your festive entertaining.

Using the basic pattern provided, you can create as detailed a sleigh as you wish. Christmas cards, books and magazines are a great source of ideas for different designs of sleighs. Reindeer cut-outs can also be placed in front of the sleigh to create a larger full-length piece, if you have time (and the space available).

A Christmas sleigh filled to overflowing with rich, dark and white chocolate truffles creates a sophisticated and irresistible display box. For children, you could add coloured sweets and candies. An attractive addition would be to cut out and decorate a Father Christmas figure and reindeer, to position alongside the sleigh. Tiny wrapped gifts, if they are not too heavy, could also be put inside.

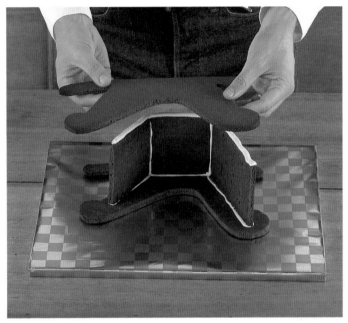

1 Cut out card templates to the dimensions required, and make the gingerbread pieces. You will need 2 side sleigh pieces; 1 square for the bottom; and 1 long and 1 short rectangle for the back and front (see page 117 for the outlines, and page 20 on how to trace and make card templates).

3 Continue by piping a line of icing along the left-hand edge and bottom of the front rectangle. Place it on at an angle, as with the back.

With these 3 pieces standing, pipe a line of icing along all the upper edges and press the other side of the sleigh gently into place. It is best to leave this construction to dry for 24 hours before setting it upright.

2 To begin, lay 1 of the scalloped sides of the sleigh down flat. Taking the longer of the 2 rectangles (the back of the sleigh), pipe a line of royal icing along the right side and bottom of that piece and place it long-side down at right angles to the shaped side piece.

Next, pipe a line of icing along the right side of the bottom square and place along the base of the sleigh, attaching it to the back piece already in position.

4 Using a spatula, swirl a thin layer of white royal icing on the cake board leaving 1 in/2.5 cm from the edge uncovered to allow for 'thumb room'. Before the royal icing 'snow' begins to set, lift your sleigh from its side and stand it up at an angle on the cake board.

5 Using brown royal icing, pipe stars on the bottom runners of the sleigh following the star fill-in method. Using green and red royal icing, pipe trails of holly leaves and red berries along the back curve and front curve of each side of the sleigh. You may also choose to accent the sides with red scrolls. Trim all edges of the sleigh with ivory-coloured royal icing, using the shell border technique. All the above piping techniques are shown on page 25.

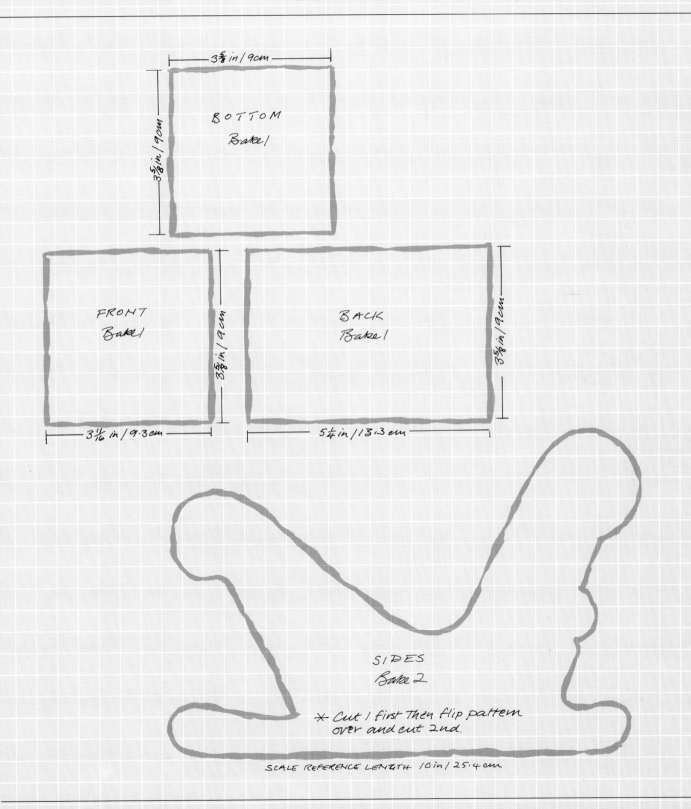

BOTTOM
Bake 1

3⅝ in / 9 cm

3⅝ in / 9 cm

FRONT
Bake 1

3⅝ in / 9 cm

3 1/16 in / 9.3 cm

BACK
Bake 1

3⅝ in / 9 cm

5¼ in / 13.3 cm

SIDES
Bake 2

* Cut 1 first then flip pattern
over and cut 2nd.

SCALE REFERENCE LENGTH 10 in / 25.4 cm

Haunted House

T his house of terror is sure to scare all the little ghosts and goblins trick or treating on Hallowe'en. To add a really mystical effect, you can even put a small light-bulb inside, threading the wire through the bottom of the centre of the cake board before assembling the house around it. Then, with the room lights off and the haunted house lit up, an eerie glow will come from the windows.

Decorating this house can be great fun, as it is meant to be dilapidated and run-down, and so does not have to be as exact as usual. The shutters are deliberately crooked, scraps of sheet gelatine are used for the windows so that they look broken, and cereal square 'tiles' are added to the roof randomly to give the impression that they are falling off.

REQUIREMENTS
gingerbread pieces made with
1 × quantity of recipe 2 (page 15)
12 in × 15 in board, covered with foil paper
6 cups/2½lb/1.1kg royal icing:
3 cups/1¼lb/550g gooseberry or moss green
2¼ cups/14oz/400g brown
½ cup/¼oz/100g white
¼ cup/2oz/50g orange
sheet gelatine (for the windows)
red and black jelly beans (for the shutters and pathway)
4 cups/1lb/450g cereal squares (for the shingles)
½ cup/3oz/85g brown sugar (for the graves)
ice-cream cone (for the tree)
marshmallow (for the bush)

A spectacular abandoned haunted house for Hallowe'en – the walls look as if they are tumbling down, the doors and shutters are crooked, and the roof tiles are falling off. Autumnal colours of brown, red and pumpkin orange add to the atmosphere. An alternative to the white ghost could be to pipe thin 'skeleton' lines on to a dark brown gingerbread man.

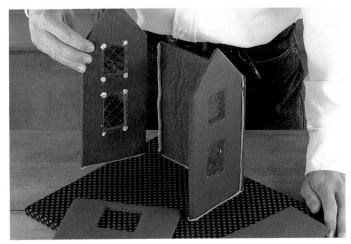

1 Cut out card templates to the dimensions required, and make the gingerbread pieces. You will need 1 front piece with holes for 2 windows and a door; a plain back piece (not shown above); 2 identical side pieces with holes for 2 windows; 2 rectangles for the roof, one with an indentation; 4 pieces, 2 with V-shaped cut-outs, for the chimney; 2 triangles for the gable roof; 2 door pieces; 12 shutters; 2 rectangles, 1 thin and 1 wide, for the steps; 2–3 arched tombstones; and 1 ghost cut-out (see page 121 for the outlines, and page 20 for how to trace and make card templates).

2 First make the windows by applying sheet gelatine to the backs of the walls over the holes (see page 27 for techniques). For these windows I actually ripped the gelatine in half and just placed the one half on, to give the look of broken windows. Then pipe a medium line of icing on the bottom edge of the back piece and attach it to the rear left-hand corner of the board. Pipe a medium line of icing on the bottom and one side of a wall piece, and place it in position; continue in the same way for the opposite wall.

3 Pipe a thin line of icing on both front edges of the side walls. Then pipe a line of icing along the bottom edge of the front wall and place it in.

Pipe a medium line of icing around the back top edges of the walls and place the complete roof piece on at the back. Next, ice on the roof piece with its slot fitting behind the pointed part of the front wall.

Assemble the chimney. Start by placing one of the sides with the V-shaped slot down on the roof. Then place the 2 square pieces on the front and back, at right angles to the roof slope. Add with the other slotted side.

Place the 2 gable roof pieces on with the shortest sides forward, resting on the pointed attic part of the front wall.

Steps are added by securing the larger of the 2 rectangles down on the board with a dab of icing. The smaller one is then secured with a dab of icing towards the back of this first piece.

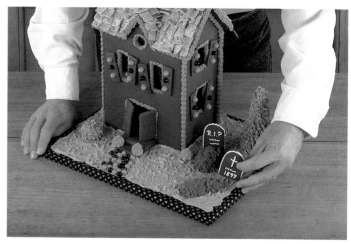

4 With brown royal icing, pipe a trim around the window and door outlines using the shell technique, and cover all the wall and chimney seams using a zig-zag border (see page 23 for techniques). Attach the doors by piping a line of royal icing on 1 long edge of each and pressing firmly on the outer edge of the opening. The doors here are deliberately hung crooked to give the effect of falling off.

Add the shutters by piping a small dab of icing behind each and pressing on gently where required. These are also placed on crooked to represent disrepair. Cut jelly beans in half with a scalpel and attach them to the shutters with a dab of icing.

Ice the roof thinly with a layer of brown royal icing and add square pieces of cereal, placing them from the bottom up, layering as you go. Don't be concerned about getting each tile on perfectly because you want an uneven effect and you have to work quickly before the icing sets.

5 Using a spatula, spread royal icing tinted a gooseberry or moss green to cover the yard area of the cake board, leaving the pathway uncovered. Once the icing is spread over, hold the spatula parallel to the board and gently tap it on the icing, lifting it up and pulling the icing to form small peaks. Using brown royal icing, spread on the pathway and pave it with jelly beans of alternating colours, cut in half, pressed gently into the icing. Pipe orange pumpkins on the door step (see page 24).

Place two mounds of brown sugar in the front yard and, with your hands, shape them into oblongs. Pipe your tombstone-shaped pieces with white lettering, and place directly in the grass at the heads of the graves. If they will not stand, brown sugar can be added behind them to keep them propped up.

Trees and shrubs can be piped (see page 26) and added to the yard as you wish.

6 Door handles are now piped on, using white royal icing and a writing tip. With the same tip, pipe on spider webs for a final scary effect (see page 23 for techniques).

7 The ghost cut-out has been smoothed with white royal icing and trimmed with an edge of dots, also of white icing. Two brown dots were then added for the eyes. With a dab of icing piped on the back, it can then be stuck to the house where desired. A ghost could also rise from the chimney if you want to make another.

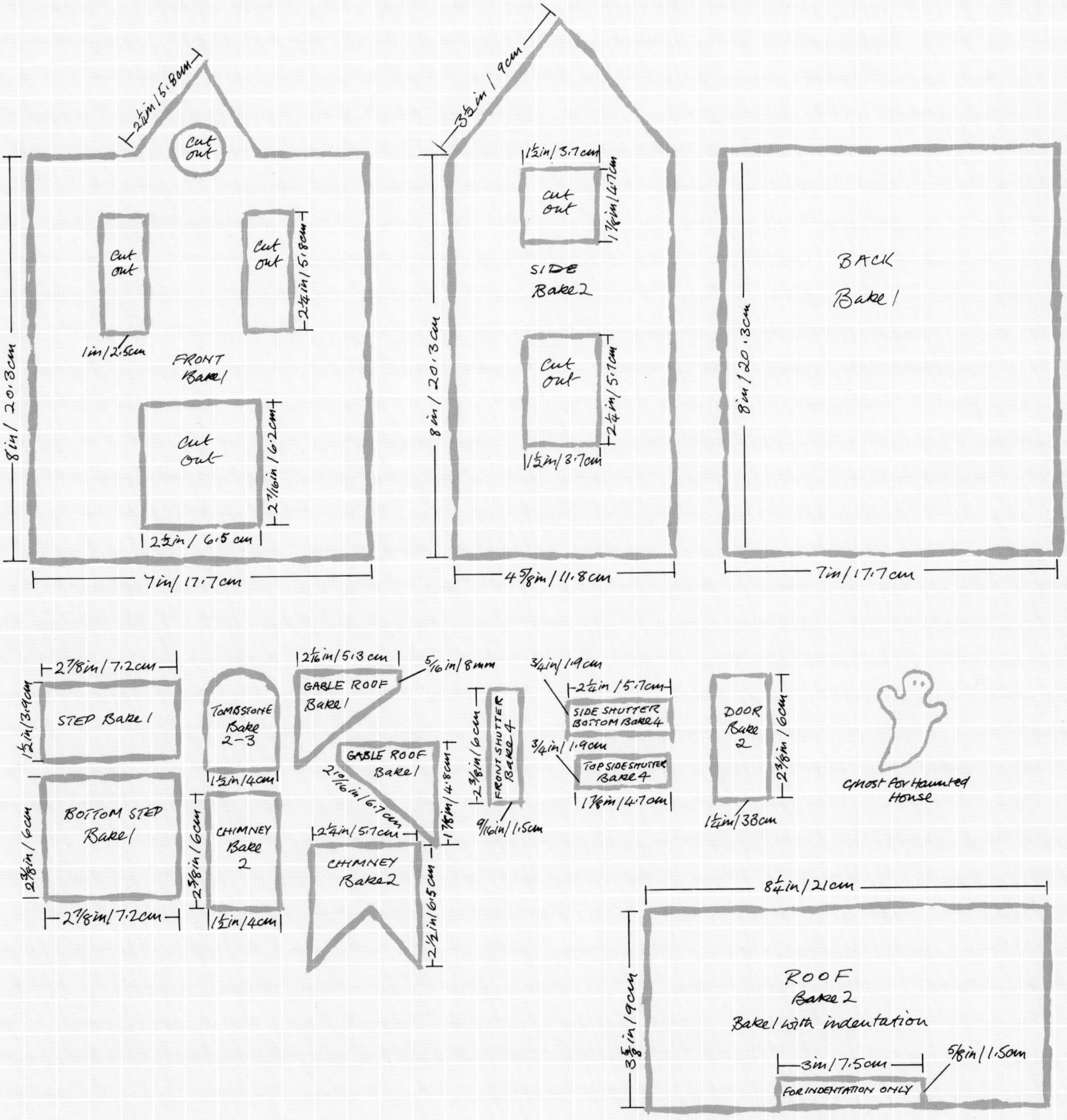
2¼in/5.8cm
Cut out
Cut out
Cut out
2¼in/5.8cm
1in/2.5cm
FRONT Bake 1
8in/20.3cm
Cut out
2 7/16in/6.2cm
2½in/6.5cm
7in/17.7cm
3½in/9cm
1½in/3.7cm
Cut out
1 7/8in/4.7cm
SIDE Bake 2
8in/20.3cm
Cut out
2¼in/5.7cm
1½in/3.7cm
4 5/8in/11.8cm
BACK Bake 1
8in/20.3cm
7in/17.7cm
2 7/8in/7.2cm
1½in/3.9cm
STEP Bake 1
BOTTOM STEP Bake 1
2 3/8in/6cm
2 7/8in/7.2cm
TOMBSTONE Bake 2–3
1½in/4cm
CHIMNEY Bake 2
2 3/8in/6cm
1½in/4cm
2 1/16in/5.3cm
5/16in/8mm
GABLE ROOF Bake 1
GABLE ROOF Bake 1
2 5/16in/6.7cm
1 7/8in/4.8cm
2¼in/5.7cm
CHIMNEY Bake 2
2½in/6.5cm
2 3/8in/6cm
FRONT SHUTTER Bake 4
9/16in/1.5cm
3/4in/1.9cm
2¼in/5.7cm
SIDE SHUTTER BOTTOM Bake 4
3/4in/1.9cm
TOP SIDE SHUTTER Bake 4
1 7/8in/4.7cm
DOOR Bake 2
2 3/8in/6cm
1½in/38cm
Ghost for Haunted House
8¼in/21cm
ROOF Bake 2
Bake 1 with indentation
3in/7.5cm
5/8in/1.5cm
FOR INDENTATION ONLY
3 5/8in/9cm

Preserving Your Gingerbread Project

There is so much planning and creativity involved in building a gingerbread masterpiece, that it is quite common to feel a strong sense of personal accomplishment once your project has been completed. If you then feel that you cannot bear to part with your creation, you may decide that it should be kept from year to year rather than be allowed to fall prey to hungry children, or even sweet-toothed adults. With the proper treatment, any gingerbread project can be preserved to give pleasure for years to come.

The two essential factors for the lasting preservation of your gingerbread are proper care and good storage. The caring starts immediately after your project has been completed, when it is first displayed. Firstly, and most importantly, place your project out of the reach of children. I have seen several gingerbread houses fall victim to children unable to resist temptation – a complete row of candies taken from the roof and a front door suddenly disappearing. So be careful of those tiny hands – they move fast.

After children, humidity is one of the most destructive elements, so always be on your guard against it. To protect your project from humidity, a clear protective edible glaze may be applied to seal the surface. Such 'confectioners' glaze' is widely available at most cake decorating and baking stores. Allow about 48 hours for your project to set thoroughly before applying any glaze. Use a medium flat brush to paint on a thin layer of the glaze, covering as much of the project as possible. When dry, the glaze will remain glossy and shiny, and does not dull in any way. Once the glaze is brushed on and still wet, it is best to leave the project for 24–48 hours to dry completely before touching or moving it as the glaze will be sticky for some time and you may smudge or smear the surface.

It is also possible to spray a project with a ceramic spray instead of using edible confectioners' glaze. However, these are toxic and will render your once-edible gingerbread creation totally inedible forever. If this type of spray is used, caution must be exercised, especially with children, who may still be tempted to take a goody thinking that it is still edible. Personally, I do not like using toxic spray and find using the edible glaze much more satisfying, knowing that the project will be preserved yet will still be safe to eat for some time to come. Once sprayed with confectioners' glaze, the project should last for up to three years. Without any protection, depending on the humidity, a project can last from three to six months.

The other essential factor in the preservation of your gingerbread project is proper storage. Again, humidity is a problem as moisture from the atmosphere will soften the gingerbread and ultimately lead to its collapse in a matter of hours. It will also make any hard candies or sweets decorating your gingerbread run and melt. To prevent this happening it is best to store your project in a cool dry place, such as a clothes closet, pantry or cupboard. Avoid basements or cellars: even though the temperature in these places is cool, the humidity level is usually high.

When you put your project in storage, place it in a cardboard box with a cardboard lid or covered with fabric or a thin plastic bag. This will prevent dust from collecting on the piece and will preserve your project in all its glory, so that it will look as good as new when it is unpacked.

SUPPLIERS

Ingredients for making gingerbread can be found from most grocers but for obtaining specialist decorating supplies the following list might be helpful:

United Kingdom

The British Sugarcraft Guild
Wellington House, Messeter Place, Eltham, London SE9 5DP. 081 859 6943.

The House of Sugarcraft
Suppliers of flower cutters, powder and paste colours and piping tubes. Unit 10, Broxhead Industrial Estate, Lindford Road, Bordon, Hampshire GU35 0NY.

Cake Art Ltd
Wholesale suppliers of icings and equipment. Unit 16, Crown Close, Crown Industrial Estate, Priors Wood, Taunton, Somerset TA2 8RX.

Sugarcraft Supplies PME (Harrow) Ltd
Suppliers of decorating equipment. Brember Road, South Harrow, Middlesex HA2 8UN.

JF Renshaw Ltd
Suppliers of icings. Locks Lane, Mitcham, Surrey CR4 2XG.

Jenny Campbell Trading/BR Matthews and Son
12 Gypsy Hill, Upper Norwood, London SE19 1NN.

Mary Ford Cake Artistry Centre Ltd
28–30 Southbourne Grove, Southbourne, Bournemouth, Dorset BH6 3RA.

Woodnutts Ltd
97 Church Road, Hove, Sussex BN3 2BA.

Essex Icing Centre
20 Western Road, Billericay, Essex CM12 9DZ.

Sugarworks
161 Lower High Street, Stourbridge, West Midlands, DY8 1TS.

Squires Kitchen
Squires House, 3 Waverley Lane, Farnham, Surrey, GU9 8BB.

House of Cakes
18 Meadow Close, Woodley, Stockport, Cheshire, SK6 1QZ.

North America

ICES (International Cake Exploration Society)
membership enquiries:
3087–30th St. S.W., Ste.101, Grandville, Michigan 49418.

Maid of Scandinavia
(equipment, supplies, courses, magazine *Mailbox News*)
3244 Raleigh Avenue, Minneapolis, Minnesota 55416.

Wilton Enterprises Inc
2240 West 75th Street, Woodridge, Illinois 60517.

Home Cake Artistry Inc
1002 North Central, Suite 511, Richardson, Texas 75080.

Lorraine's Inc
148 Broadway, Hanover, Massachusetts 02339.

McCall's School of Cake Decorating Inc
3810 Bloor Street West, Islington, Ontario, Canada, M9B 6C2.

Australia

Australian National Cake Decorators' Association
PO Box 321, Plympton, South Australia 5038.

Cake Decorating Association of Victoria
President, Shirley Vaas, 4 Northcote Road, Ocean Grove, Victoria 3226.

Cake Decorating Guild of New South Wales
President, Fay Gardiner, 4 Horsley Cres, Melba, Act, New South Wales 2615.

Cake Decorating Association of Tasmania
Secretary, Jenny Davis, 29 Honolulu Street, Midway Point, Tasmania 7171.

Cake Decorators' Association of South Australia
Secretary, Lorraine Joliffe, Pindari, 12 Sussex Crescent, Morphet Vale, South Australia 5162.

Fer Lewis, Cake Ornament Company
156 Alfred Street, Fortitude Valley, Brisbane 4006.

New Zealand

New Zealand Cake Decorators Guild
Secretary, Morag Scott, 17 Ranui Terrace, Tawa, Wellington.

Decor Cakes
RSA Arcade, 435 Great South Road, Otahaha.

South Africa

South African Sugarcraft Guild
National Office, 1 Tuzla Mews, 187 Smit Street, Fairlan 2195.

INDEX

I would like to thank the following people for their help and support during the production of this book: my lovely wife Deb for her patience, love and support; my darling daughter Jenna for the sweet and memorable telephone conversations I had with her while I was away; my mother and father for the many long-distance phone calls of love and understanding; Bill and Deloris with the endless cards of support; Gary and Colin for allowing me to disrupt their home with gingerbread pieces and for reorganizing the kitchen so that nothing could be found; Nick and Janet for their never-ending friendship and the fun-filled shopping sprees needed to keep me going; and Janet back home for fulfilling certain cake-decorating commitments and for keeping the shops in business during my absence. Thanks also to all my friends in I.C.E.S. and the British Sugarcraft Guild for their encouragement, and to the special team Carole, Cortina, Joanna, Heather, Alan, Jacqui and Isabel who made this book a reality.

The author and publishers would like to thank Anne Nicol for baking the gingerbread, and the following for kindly loaning material for some of the photographs in this book: The Shaker Shop, 25 Harcourt Street, London W1; Cortell and Barratt, 40 High Street, Ewell Village, Surrey; Knightsbridge Bakeware, Cheltenham, Glos.; Joan Mooney; The Brown Bag Cookie Mould Company, Unit 30–31, Wodsbridge Industrial Estate, Three-Legged Cross, Dorset; Bentalls, Kingston-upon-Thames, Surrey; and The House of Sugarcraft, Unit 10, Broxhead Industrial Estate, Lindford Road, Bordon, Hampshire.